Charles Henry Crandall

The Chords of Life

Poems

Charles Henry Crandall

The Chords of Life
Poems

ISBN/EAN: 9783744704427

Printed in Europe, USA, Canada, Australia, Japan

Cover: Foto ©Thomas Meinert / pixelio.de

More available books at **www.hansebooks.com**

"Round which Ondawa idly loves to linger,
Wearing her weirs like gems upon her finger."

—*A Country Town.*

The Chords of Life

POEMS

BY

Charles H. Crandall

> By the heart must be expended
> What shall work upon the heart
> — *Goethe*

PRINTED FOR THE AUTHOR
SPRINGDALE, CONN.
1898.

Copyright, 1897
by
CHARLES H. CRANDALL

DEDICATED TO FOUR LITTLE LADS

Arthur — Robert — Roland — Clarence

CONTENTS

SOME LONGER POEMS

	PAGE
The Chords of Life	11
In Nature's Kindergarten School	12
Love Forever	13
I Asked for Beauty	14
A Country Town	15
A September Gale	17
The Fall of the Leaves	18
In Autumn-Tide	21
In Snow Time	24
Lost Melodies	25
The School Teacher	27
An Easter Picture	32
Conscience	34
To Nature	37
The Record of Happiness	39
Dutche Towne Girles	40
The Beggar Maid	43
A Hymn to Ponus	49
Greeting to Stamford	51

LYRICS OF LIFE

Peace Vale	55
Christmas Emblems	56
Instruments	56
A Farewell to Yesterday	57
Where Shall We Bury Him?	58
The Bridge	59
Gerardia	60
"Heimgang"	60
The Voyage	61
The Return of the Ship	61
Creeds	62
The Over-curtain	63

CONTENTS

	PAGE
City Parks	64
To L. E. S. and E. B. S.	64
Birds of Passage	65
The Poet	65
On Fort Greene	66
When This Shall Be Dream	67
To-morrow	68
The Coming Poet	69
Argonauts	70
To James Whitcomb Riley	71
To a Mouse at a Ball	72
The Cycle	73
Crossing East River Bridge	74
Quatrains	74
Concord	75
Thomas Carlyle	76
Requiem	77
In Memoriam	78

SONGS AND LOVE LYRICS

Spring Song	80
Sweetheart, Be True	80
Oh, Look From Out the Starry Skies	81
An Old-Fashioned Song	82
A Meadow Serenade	83
A Sea Song	84
When Love Doth Lie A-Dreaming	85
Heart to Heart	85
Angel Heart	86
With Lilacs	86
Capitulation	87
Columbia	87
A Desire	88
Her Little Foot	89
Four Guardsmen	90

CONTENTS

	PAGE
The Tryst	90
My Riddle	92
A Gift Too Grand	93
Sanctuary	94
The Music Cure	95
Love	96
Among the Daisies	97
At Lake George	98
An Evolution	99
Crossing Ontario	99
A Loving Cup	100
A Visit from the Muse	100
The Offer	102

SONNETS

In Midsummer	103
The Sonnet's Chime	103
Asters and Goldenrod	104
May and June	104
One I Know	105
Creasy's Fifteen Battles	106
By the Burned Dwelling	106
Wilhelmj	107
Conscience	107
Often I Leave Thee	108
Mary Anderson	108
To Venus	109

POEMS OF HOME-LIFE, ETC.

An Hour of Song	110
Old-Fashioned Flowers	111
Our Round Table	112
Lines	113
Baby's Paradise	114
To a Sparrow	114

CONTENTS

	PAGE
Trust	115
A Diamond	116
Stella	116
To Clarise	117
Two Sisters	118
A Silver Wedding	119
A Golden Wedding	120
Thanksgiving Day	121
The Fresh Air Children	122
Tick-Tock	122

FARM POEMS, DIALECT, ETC.

Plowing	124
A Song of the Drudge	128
"The Last Day of School"	130
No Paradise for Animals	133
Jennie B.	134
Driving the Colt	137
Told in the Basin	138
The Hornin'	143

PATRIOTIC VERSE

Then and Now	146
Washington	147
Grant	148
A Knight of Gold	149
Election Day	150
Cuba Libre	150
A Soldier's Song	152
Progress	153
At Greeley's Grave	154
Integer Vitæ	155

LIST OF ILLUSTRATIONS

	PAGE
Fair Greenwich (*Frontispiece*)	
Lost Melodies ("*Adagio*," by *von Hoessler*)	25
Ponus Monument	49
Rippowam River	55
The Reaper	103
An Hour of Song	110

SOME LONGER POEMS

THE CHORDS OF LIFE

OH, touch me a strain on the Chords of Life,
    Careless, and fresh, and sweet;
For youth is gazing with dewy eye,
And a bird on the bough sings merrily,
    And the blossoms fall at our feet.
Then dance and carol a roundelay,
Like fairies that usher a feast in May,
A song that's fit for the baby's ear,
While the lilies shall laugh and lean to hear
    What the zephyr may have to say.
        Touch fleet!
        Touch sweet!
    Like fairies that feast in May.

Oh, strike me a strain on the Chords of Life,
    Martial, and strong, and brave;
As the gale and the forest in glorious strife,
    Or the storm-cloud kissing the wave.
For life is at noon and the stress is sweet,
And we march to the sound of hurrying feet;
A time for doing, a time for wooing,
In hall and cottage brave hearts are suing;
There's a call to arms in the lady's glance,
And the knight rides forth with level lance.
Then sweep the strings with a music bold,
Waken the songs of the days of old,
    And echo them o'er the land!
        Strike strong!
        Strike long!
    Oh, strike with a kingly hand!

Oh, gently now on the Chords of Life,
    Gently, and sad, and slow!
Age is watching the paling sky,

The red leaves flutter swiftly by,
  And the back-log smoulders low.
Glamor of childhood, yet more deep,
Comes back now by the hearth to sleep;
Faintly echoes the battle-call,
The sword hangs idly on the wall;
There's a patter of wolfish feet
Where the frost-pack follows fleet,
And we sit by the dreaming fire —
Silence our one desire.
            Strike low!
            Strike slow!
    Silence our one desire!

IN NATURE'S KINDERGARTEN SCHOOL

IN Nature's kindergarten school
    I gather out of grass and dew —
Emblem of her eternal rule —
    A cup and saucer, brown of hue.

An acorn? Yes. And as I gaze,
    From wheels of chariots, spoke on spoke
The sunlight falls in glittering rays
    That praise the product of the oak!

Heart of the acorn! Heart of me!
    Which is the lesser, which more blind?
The germ that longs to be a tree
    Or I who yearn toward humankind?

Whether we will it so or not,
    Time teaches both that it is best
To long, aspire — to grasp our lot —
    To strive and suffer — and to rest.

O kindly rule, that, of the seed,
    Imprisoned in its brown cup shell,

Ne'er asks that it be oak or reed,
   But just to grow, and all is well!

O sweet content in lowly ways,
   That bids the soul to strike no note
To jar with unexacted lays
   That well up in the robin's throat!

So will our dream of dreams come true.
   From seeds we cannot see to-day,
Out of the old shall come the new,
   Out of the dark the morning ray.

LOVE FOREVER

YES, the gods are dumb and dead,
   But the bobolink sings on!
And the bluebird, overhead,
Pipes his joy when Day has won
Fair Aurora's blushing face,
Hidden in a cloudy lace.
While the pipe of Pan is still,
Let the new world have its will!
Listen to the robin's playing,
On the maple's top a-swaying,
Ah, so proud of that one nest, —
Puffing out his scarlet vest, —
Piper of the dress parade
In sunrise glow or twilight shade.

Yes, the gods are dumb and dead;
Never naiad from the rushes
Shrieks at panting faun that pushes
Through the bushes where she sped.
But a maid can charm us now,
Sitting 'neath the apple bough,
Where the snowy blossoms flying

Mingle with the music sighing,
And the petals of her song
By the breeze are borne along.
Lovers by the trysting tree
Care not if they never see
Chaste Diana on the lea;
Roaming round the firefly camp
They shall covet not the lamp
Psyche carried through the damp.

Whispering to his bashful love,
Every lover seems a Jove,
Stooping from some sphere above.
So the maiden in the morn
Seemeth to the swain, love-lorn,
Venus, from the sea, new-born!
What if gods are dumb and dead,
So that Love lives on instead,
And the roses touch and wed?

I ASKED FOR BEAUTY

I ASKED for Beauty, and heard reply,
"There's naught so far, there's naught so nigh."

I prayed to Beauty, and she was kind;
She gave me seeing, who erst was blind.

Her rays, reflected, all things did dart
Through eye and ear, through mind and heart.

I said, Sweet spirit, some gift I'd give.
"I ask no gift but the life you live."

Then rest you, Beauty, nor journey afar.
"Each night I fly from the farthest star."

Yet, near us, sometimes, are you hid?
"Perhaps I sleep 'neath a coffin lid."

But oft you vanish in cloud that clings.
"The pure in heart shall see all things."

Know you of Goodness, of Truth, and Love?
"They climb the stair to the One above."

Why, of the sisters, are you most fair?
"Their blended grace is the robe I wear."

This heart, all melted, your slave will be!
"Nay, I have loved you, and made you free."

A COUNTRY TOWN
(Greenwich, N. Y.)

"SWEET Auburn, loveliest village of the plain!"
    Thus Goldsmith sang in ever-beauteous strain;
Nor can I sing — without a throb that thrills —
My native village in the northern hills,
Round which Ondawa loves to sweetly linger,
Wearing her weirs like gems upon her finger.
Oft have I paused upon the bridge to note
The spray from many a cataract upfloat.
Veiling like incense now the village spires,
Lifting up, too, the loiterer's desires.
Often again where silent stretches sweep,
Telling where waters journey still and deep,
Gladly I've watched the bass among the rocks,
Or, in the water, seen the fleecy flocks
Of those blue heavens journeying along —
Fair as a love thought mirrored in a song!

While the stout yeomen bind the bearded grain,
Or through thy valleys drive the loaded wain;

While the white sheep take their reluctant way
Down to thy ponds, each annual washing day;
While thy proud steeds uplift the neigh that thrills;
While low thy cattle on thy thousand hills;
While from thy whirring wheels and spindles come
The welcome sounds of labor's busy hum;
While laddie's shout meets answering lassie's smile,
In happy comradeship that knows no guile;
While in thy schools is lit the inspiring flame
Of emulation on the road to fame;
While from thy churches float upon the air
Thy people's voices, blended song and prayer,
There is no need my pen thy charms should tell —
Thy beauties praise thee, and they praise thee well!

On Willard's Mount the patriot eye may see
The beacons blaze again for liberty;
Again the guns of Saratoga boom,
A nation's birth-hour and a tyrant's doom!
As hills and vales and streamlets rise again
In fair mirage on Memory's misty plain,
Often the wanderer's mind will speak thy name
To conjure up Youth's lost, bewitching flame;
Oft will the fancy of the rover think
He drinks thy streamlets, bending to the brink;
Or stealing, stealthy, to some tortuous glen,
Spies where the wily trout doth make his den;
Or when the stream, in icy armor dight,
Calls youth and maidens in the glittering night,
Then shall he don the swiftly gliding steel
And all of romance, all of beauty feel.

What matters if thy name be writ in books?
Thy mountains praise thee and thy pearly brooks.

Little can man add to thy royal share
Whom God and Nature made so passing fair.
Only for us to learn the lesson well —
No weirs can glisten in a streamless dell,
No mill-wheels turn unless the stream shall flow,
Nor river run unless the forests grow.
The Hudson rises in each tiny spring
That to its bosom gives an offering;
And civic greatness has no other start
Than simple virtue in each single heart.

A SEPTEMBER GALE

SWOOPING over the corn-fields,
   Blowing their tepees awry,
Whirling the crows in hundreds,
   Like leaves, against the sky,
Veering and beating and darting —
   Would that I, too, might fly!

Over the uplands together,
   Wander at will and sing!
This is the care-free weather —
   Make the blue welkin ring!
For the gale has broken its tether,
   And the wind is a living thing!

Towns and cities and peoples
   Helpless lie in thy way.
Shake all their towers and steeples,
   Strain every topmast and stay,
Blow all our poor human error
   Far o'er the buffeted bay!

Roar, thou viking of heaven!
   Whistle thy songs uncouth;
Drive back the dallying breezes
   Into the lap of the South;
Start all the forest to war tunes
   With blasts from thy mighty mouth.

Aye, walls and chimneys must crumble,
   And people but haste to decay;
The kingdoms totter and tumble
   And are blown with a storm breath away;
So, with roar and laughter and rumble,
   Ride on, thou king of a day!

Yea, I am thy subject, as loyal
   As the asters that bend in thy path,
And the goldenrod — messengers royal —
   Or scent of the late aftermath.
I fill my lungs at thy bellows
   And share in thy boisterous wrath.

My arms are spread like the oak tree
   To welcome thy lusty embrace;
I scud with the gusts, bareheaded,
   And exult in thy glorious race;
For the autumn wind is my lover,
   And I welcome him, face to face.

THE FALL OF THE LEAVES
(An Autumn Reverie.)

BORNE on the breath of morn,
   Wafted by winds of night,
Eddying here,
Scattering there,
Leaving the boughs forlorn,

THE FALL OF THE LEAVES

Making the hollows bright,
Mother Earth calling
Them to their falling —
Falling leaves!

Hark to their music sweet;
Sweet and sad as they pass
Through the thick web
Of twigs overhead,
Tinkling on boughs they meet,
Raining down on the grass,
Gleaming so brightly,
Dropping so lightly —
Watch the leaves!

Sadly the gray sky grieves
O'er the summer fallen and dead;
And the north wind rough,
Takes the beautiful woof,
And into the dry grass weaves
A carpet a king might tread.
From mountain to strand,
All over the land,—
Falling leaves!

Like a flock of bright-winged birds
They are fluttering down from the trees,
Never again to fly
Their beauty in the sky.
Never again will be heard
Their song on the wandering breeze,
Soothing the souls of men,
Whispering over again
Message sweet.

Yet other leaves will come,
And glow, and fade, and fall;
And other eyes shall see
Their beauty on the tree,

And the maidens bring them home
To deck the cottage wall;
While over the lawn
The children run,
Tossing the leaves —
Happy leaves!

They fall like the tribes of men,
As they hurry down to their graves;
Beaten by every blast,
They sink to their rest at last;
And they never will live again,
Vanished to mix with the leaves
That through the long years
Have fallen like tears —
Nature's tears.

And still come the airy hosts,
Pouring their strength on the ground.
Soon they will be at rest,
Close in their dark graves prest;
Yet a few, in the winter, like ghosts,
Will fly with a rustling sound
Round the safe dwelling,
Their mournful tale telling —
Withered leaves!

I think o'er the fall of friends
As I muse o'er the fall of the year;
And the air is filled
With the thoughts distilled,
And my song of the autumn ends,
And I mark the close with a tear,
Then fling my pen far away,
And all the rest of the day
Watch the leaves,
Falling leaves.

AUTUMN-TIDE

UP! Away from toil and care,
While the frost is in the air
Send the sluggard, Sleep, away,
Do not fear his overstay.
Hurry, or we miss the morning
Helios is now adorning.
See, he shakes his golden head
As he rises from his bed!
Ah! His pillow was a hill,
Fringed with silver at his will,
And the clouds he had for cover
Golden-canopied him over!
Speed, thou ruler of the day,
We, too, shall be bright and gay!
To the future, future cast,
To oblivion the past.
For to-day we'll lose ourselves
And be like the fays and elves;
Caring not for latitude,
We shall make our home the wood.

Let your dress be light and airy,
So they'll take you for a fairy,
And my cloak, too, shall be humble,
Ready for a roll or tumble.
Lightly o'er the meadows pass,
Brushing hoar-frost from the grass,—
Leaping o'er the orchard walls,
Where the fragrant fruitage falls,
Lying ruddy at our feet,
Making all the region sweet.
See! a hearth smoke stains the sky,
And a milkmaid, tripping by,
Musically calls the kine
Where they stand in patient line,

Waiting till she drops the bars.
Now a horn the silence mars,
And a house-dog's deep alarm
Sounds across from yonder farm.

But away, away from these;
Our companions are the trees.
We shall find the talking oak
And the burning bush that spoke.
We will argue with the rills,
Hold communion with the hills,
See the Autumn's warm desires
Burning in her mountain fires.
Aught but Nature's foreign land,
Men we cannot understand;
For we are as newly born
And to-day's our natal morn.
Featly now we clear the stiles,
Press, unweary, on for miles,
Where yon forest-garnished dome
Smiles and beckons, saying, "Come!"

Now the mountains lock us round,
And one scarce can hear a sound
That the solitude dispels,
Save the tinkle of the bells,
Where the woolly legions stray
Round the sheepfold, far away.
In this hill-encircled valley
All the nymphs and naiads rally;
And unless our eyes are stupid
We shall get a glimpse of Cupid
Sleeping on his golden bow —
Psyche o'er him bending low.
Only yonder is the shade
Where the coy Sabbrina strayed.

AUTUMN-TIDE

She has left some lilies there,
Where she lately decked her hair.
Listen! that is Pan, indeed!
Don't you recognize the reed?
Seeking wood-sprites? Here you find them,
Casting saucy looks behind them,
Throwing chestnuts — aren't they jolly?
Give them volley back for volley!
There they frolic in yon hollow.
Up! Away, and quickly follow.

Let us rest upon the leaves,
Listen while the brooklet grieves.
Watch the waves, with leaves at play,
Eddy, plunge, and whirl away;
Note the hawk, with restless eye,
Draw his circles on the sky.
What's this clamor now that greets?
'Tis the crows in airy fleets
Convoyed by their wisest bird,
His ragged pinions faintly heard.
Now has died their carping din,
And like some great strange violin,
The wind draws on the pine his bow,
And makes a music, sweet and low.

Come! A charge at yonder hill!
We'll take the fortress with a will.
Ranks of hickory, birch, and oak
At our onslaught quickly broke!
We have gained the mountain crest,
And have earned our glorious rest.
Clouds, that journey through the blue,
Take our thoughts along with you;
Winds, that now our temples greet,
Bring them back as pure and sweet.

Fill the lungs and bare the head,
The world is live that late was dead.
Now for greater views of life,
Now new courage for its strife.
From your eye dismiss the mote,
Let your soul outgrow your coat.
Then the cataract that calls
From Diondehowa's Falls,
Stream and lake and distant hill,
Surpliced mountain peaks that fill
Priestly office, sky and cloud
Shall whisper, sing, and speak aloud;
Call and echo, still, again :
Benediction and Amen.

IN SNOW TIME

'TWAS sung by a poet of long ago,
　　The grace and the charm of the " Beautiful Snow,"
Yet who the poet was none may know.
For the snow that falleth so soft and deep,
Safe from our eyes its poet doth keep,
Wrapped in oblivion, fast asleep!
Yet, who would not, when the north winds blow,
Sleep with the violets, safe and low,
Lulled and hushed by the motherly snow?
So I think as the flakes go by,
White as angels, down from the sky,
Folded safe in the fields to lie,
A peace comes down with the winter's white
That seems to set all the old world right,
A charity, pure, and wide, and bright.
Then there comes in the taste of the air,
A zest and sparkle that's sweet and rare,
That draws the stings and the hurts of care.

"LOST MELODIES."

The woods are a forest of coral white,
The fences are Alps of mimic height,
With crests and arabesques all bedight!
Glows then gather in evening's skies,
Hints of the soul's divine emprise,
So soft and blending the color lies;
Lavender, gray, and purple hues,
Gold and ruby, the west suffuse,
Rarer than ever in summer's dews.
What though the diamond melts as it warms,
Now, on my hand, yet the beautiful forms
Tell of the wealth of the God of storms!
Thus the flakes that softly alight,
Turning the earth to a faery sight,
Tell of a power to make pure and white
Even the souls in the thrall of sin,
Bidding His white peace enter in,
Bidding His reign of love begin.
So it is, when I hear the sound
Of merry sleigh-bells echoing round,
That the earth still smiles, though snowy gowned!
And I say with reverence, whispered low, —
Say with the poet of years ago, —
Beautiful, beautiful, beautiful snow!

LOST MELODIES

YOU who have heard a world-loved singer winging
   On white, clear tones up to the arch of Joy,
Oh, wonder now what may have been her singing
   When, all alone, and free from all annoy,
      On some still morning's air
         She opened up her heart,
      Singing beyond compare,
         Forgetting it was art!

Not to be courted in the crowded street,
  But shyly, to the artist comes his Art.
No tongue must tell to common ears how sweet
  Her smile can be when they withdraw apart.
      The minstrel's highest songs
        Are sung to skies and hills;
      He unto Song belongs,
        But Song flies as she wills.

Ah, when a strain is struggling in the heart,
  Then bursts and wings in melody divine,—
Who'll catch the truant, once it has a start?
  Let loose the falcon Thought! It may be thine!
      Bribe Echo for its trail,
        And harness Fancy's feet!
      Seek out this latest Grail
        With love than life more fleet!

I asked the Wind which way the vision vanished,
  I prayed the Stars to gild its flying track,
I braved the Sun, and cried: Why is it vanished?
  Their sad, blank faces drave my question back.
      Who seeks the lost Ideal —
        A bird bred not for cages?
      It tempts us toward the Real,
        In footsteps of the sages.

Lost Friend! A melody lost in a Friend!
  Thou art but as a lure to guide my groping;
Out of this labyrinth to give me trend
  Unto a realm of seeing, knowing, hoping.
      So swiftly thou didst flee
        To leave to me for dower
      Hints in each wayside tree,
        Beckonings in each flower.

And benison of little baby faces
  Drops from the skies on spirits who have known,

Bound up in miniature, all the skyey graces,
  Printed by Love, in hidden vigils lone.
    Ah, when the lisping tongue
      The last dear word had spoken!
    O little heart unstrung!
      O baby harp that's broken!

Lost Song, lost Dream, lost Friend, lost Baby fingers,—
  Shrined in a realm elusive, strangely near,—
Why chide one who, a prisoner, still lingers,
  Shut by the "dead-line" from your freedom dear?
      Yet, dreaming how you roam,
        Our steps may grow the fleeter
      To seek the mystic home
        Whose welcome you make sweeter.

THE SCHOOL TEACHER

A MISSION sought her in the crowded town;
    A call to service, like a draft to arms.
So, following Duty to the high brick walls,
Where children's voices hummed like hives of bees,
She gave her life to them, and so denied
A throng of pleasures tempting her away;
Still followed cheerily, although she knew
Necessity trod close on Duty's steps.
So, oft, Necessity will stretch one hand,
And hide, for shame, the other at her back!

A patient captain with her raw recruits,—
And some unkempt, not tidy to her taste,—
She taught the manual of mental arms,
The subtle difference betwixt "ayes" and "ahs,"

27

THE CHORDS OF LIFE

How to subdue the coltish verbs and nouns,
And learn the tricks of crooked 3's and 8's,
Those slippery clowns that sport upon the slate,
And tangle up the tender brain of youth.

So oft she told the story of the world,
Or outlined all its oceans, islands, streams;
Its divers towns from Schaghticoke to Rome;
It seemed, sometimes, the earth had really changed,
And all become a stupid, tiresome map
To weary her and little children's lives.
Oft, when the schoolroom babble reached its height,
And small, galvanic limbs beat restlessly
Upon the wooden desks or dusty floor,
And every face looked mischief, she would trace
The old Darwinian theory back, and see,
Instead of children with immortal souls,
A horde of chattering monkeys mocking her!

Yet every morn she girt her patience up,
And as she leaned her head above her desk
In hour of prayer, like a fresh flower she seemed,
And even the children gazed in wonderment.
Sometimes in sheer despair she overthrew
The bald, poor scheme of school curriculum,
And told the children stories of the stars —
Of the lost Pleiad, of Orion's chase,
The throng of sister planets, suns on suns,
That rush the light across the universe
Like torch-bearers, incredible of speed.
She made them seek at night the great north "Bear,"
And make the "Bear" point out the polar star,
And then she'd watch the wonder in their eyes
Reflected at the tale of other stars

They ne'er might see, the lovely "Southern Cross,"
The shrine of far, sub-equatorial skies,
Which flames upon that southern hemisphere.
So would she break the crust of hard routine
To get the better yield; sometimes a prize
Would offer for a bit of handiwork,
For one who made for her the smoothest rule
Or best embroidered on a bit of silk.
Sometimes the room would be transfigured. Then
The little faces glowed with tenderness,
And looking through the dross of little forms
She saw their souls, their possibilities,
And thinking of the battle and the stress
That soon would challenge all these little hearts,
She prayed anew for strength to lead them on —
On in the ways of health and noble use,
On in the ways of fearless truth and right,
On to a goal of joy and perfect peace.

Then, too, the chord of precious sympathy,
Reacting, sought the teacher from the child,
For even careless youth could not but note
The patient virtue of the one that taught.
In that soft beam when eye met tender eye
Was often forged a bond affectionate,
Of endless debt and unpaid sacrifice,
Peculiar tie, that ever must exist
Between the child and teacher. Hardly they,
The fledglings of the high, bleak city walls,
Could guess, however, that the lovely charm,
That sometimes lit her brow and changed her smile
Into a radiant light for all the room,
Was but some memory of her country home,
The peace of mountains, forest, field, and stream,
That shone reflected in her chastened face.

Each year a new brood sped, a new came in
Each year her feet and all those little ones
Wore deepening hollows in the threshold stone.
But still she kept her steadfast courage up
As if she knew her work was blessed of God,
And trusted Him in full to do His part.
She welcomed all the welcome Saturdays —
Brief respite — and the Sabbath's island calm.
Perchance, with friends, one evening in a week,
She stole a night for concert, lecture, play,
Aught to refresh, as if, her mind a slate,
She needs must sponge it, sometimes, clear of care.
And when the clover reddened in the fields
Up at her northern home, and school was done,
She hurried there to spend her well-earned rest.
Out in the fields she raked the fragrant hay,
Or trained the hollyhocks, or climbed the hills,
And in the shadow of some mighty rock,
Or where a stream sang underneath the trees,
Would read some restful book or poet's song
And dream of days when school would be no
    more.

A life monotonous! Yet memory
Had still a day to reckon from, to light
Her after skies with mingled cloud and sun.
It was one winter when the holidays
Were just o'erpast, a man came seeking her —
As men have ever gone a-seeking wives,
More apt to magnify their own desert
Than to appreciate the boon they ask.
He was a worthy man, a proper man —
They oft had met in church or Sunday school —
His manners not unkind, if sometimes rude.
Could she have loved an ordinary heart,
Just useful, not romantic in the least, —
Still manly, fair, and generous to provide, —

THE SCHOOL TEACHER

She might have stepped as from a toilsome path
Into a carriage, and have toiled no more;
But been the mistress of a good, snug house
And even the ruler of her husband's heart.
But as he wooed, in blunt, frank, tradesman way,
She seemed to hear her children calling her —
Her hundred children in the crowded school —
And so with trembling heart she put him off!

How strange it was that on that very day,
As she walked out at eve to cool her brow,
She heard a shout, and saw a crowded car,
Rounding the curve, bear down upon a boy,
A curly-headed child of Italy,
Who stood still, dazed, unknowing how to move.
Then she sprang like a deer and thrust him so
That, while he fell outside the farther rail,
Her own brave impulse carried her too far.
There was a grinding shock upon her foot —
And then the ambulance — the hospital.
When after many weeks she left the ward —
White cots, white faces, and white-aproned girls —
The doctor told her she "must have a cane."
"'Twill be a good thing," said he merrily,
"To beat off men that bother pretty girls."
So, when her wooer came again to woo,
She smiled and said she'd found a new support —
Her cane — he would not want a poor, lame wife —
The school was but a few short blocks away —
She well could walk it, with her good stout cane —
Then all her children seemed to love her so —
The little lad she saved was one of them —
So — he was kind, and she, perhaps, was wrong —
But — she made choice to give her life — to *them*.

Back to her school she limped the well-known way,
And to the other teachers gaily cried : —
"See, I have found a husband — my good cane —
So many women marry just 'poor sticks'!"
Thus, self-denied the safety of the wife,
Renouncing all the joy of motherhood,
She made her lonely pathway bloom again
With flowers of sympathy for other lives.
Tongues could but stammer, eyes grow dim with tears,
Recounting all the good deeds that she did,
While even her face seemed like a lovely flower
That haunted long the invalid's abode.
So, in the busy current of the town,
Part of its endless pathos, endless life,
Unknown, perhaps, to rich, or wise, or great,
The Teacher took her place and held her rank
In that stout army of unselfish souls
Whose lives rebloom again in other lives,
And even on earth win immortality.

AN EASTER PICTURE

BRIGHT breaks the Easter Morn on verdant fields
And leaves almost put out, while 'neath the ground,
Warmed by the wooing of the southern sun,
The tender roots of roses yet to blush
Thrill with glad life and urge to blossoming.
The cheery birds are twittering in the trees,
And saying in their sweetly foreign speech:
"Is it not strangely beautiful — this day?
Surely on such a morn men will put off
Their looks of grief and care, their wrinkles smooth,

And gaze with reverent wonder up to heaven
As in their childhood. Now a goodly sight
See coming through the interlacing streets —
Old men and matrons, youth and maidens fair,
And children, happy with their wealth of life.
For all are neatly dressed, and all bear flowers,
And as they meet and pass, with gladsome mien,
They seem to pass the greeting of the East,
Saying to all they meet: " *The Lord is risen!* "
Or answering: " *Yea, the Lord is risen indeed.*"

The high church bells are pealing forth their joy,
While all the radiant windows, set ajar,
Breathe out the incense and the sweet perfume
Of lilies massed, and banks of violets
Set round the altar. Now, through wide-thrown doors,
And up the aisles, with reverential tread,
The people move, with one desire and thought,
While from the sculptured organ's harmony
Swells out a holy music, scarce perceived,
It finds such fitting concord in the heart.
Then, too, are heard the muttered words of prayer,
The simple lesson from the wondrous book,
And sacred chants, and choruses of praise;
On bended heads the benediction falls —
The peaceful multitude regain their homes.

So glides the radiant Resurrection Morn,
And thus two thousand others, too, have passed,
And still the Wonder of the world is fresh,
And still the children smile away our doubt,
And still the stars and blossoms whisper faith.
For Death at worst is but a truce with Life,
And Love is ever mighter than Hate.
What though my thought, untired, wings its way
Back to that Garden Scene, unable still

To comprehend the great reality —
The broken tomb, the risen, regnant Lord?
Yet pity, pity on the hapless man
To whom this day has not a lesson brought,
Lifted up nearer to the Source of Peace,
From whom we are, to whom we flow again.

CONSCIENCE

AMID the rural scenes where I was born,
    Often, as fancy led my boyish feet,
I used to stray beside a mountain stream,
Which, after winding 'round among the hills,
And chafing against rocks, and tumbling down
In cataracts till it was vexed to foam,
Passed at a restful pace through quiet woods,
Whose shadows cooled its tide from shore to shore,
Until its former labor seemed forgot,
And all its deep, dark channel charmed to peace.
At last, the river left its leafy friends,
Ran brightly underneath a little bridge,
And widened far away among the fields,
Finding a thousand ways of doing good;
So journeyed on in silence to the sea.

Long years have passed since last I strolled beside
This murmuring daughter of the mountain springs,
And yet the stream is still as clear and bright
Within the precious bowers of my mind
As though I stood beside its banks to-day,—
And so the river runs on in my soul.
What does this vision teach, but that the true
And only beauty, seen by earnest souls,
Shall never die; and that all forms of good,
Which I have ever loved, shall ne'er be lost.

CONSCIENCE

Methinks I stand again beside that stream;
I hear the weird song of the waterfall,
And watch the eddies curling on their way;
Or, underneath the little arched bridge,
I pause to see the fishes dart about;
Or, haply, farther on, where all is calm,
I watch the watery mirror of the sky,
Framed by the trees, that line the bank, and leave
A widening vista of a new, bright world.
Aye, I have gazed so long within the depths
That they have lured me almost to believe
That I might find there, underneath the wave,
The true, untroubled life for which I long,
Where doubt, and sin, and partings could not
    come.
So I have thought till I have wished to leap
Down into this deep heaven, since I might
Not fly up to the lofty one above.
But calmer thought prevailed; and even now
I think I hear the hasting waters preach
A nobler lesson, for they tell of Conscience.

Thus saith the stream: "Brother, who loiterest
    here
To listen to my voice and watch my way,
Oh, look, and listen well! So shalt thou learn
A lesson better than the ones in books.
No man hath told me how to choose my path,
Nor can I see my way that lies before;
And yet the hills divide, the rocks give way,
And trees and flowers, like loving sisters, stand
On either bank, and cheer my passing by.

Yet am I not alone. There is a Power
That gently leads me on through day and night.
I see it not, and yet I feel its touch,
And love its leading. Oh, how quick I leap

To do its bidding! Turning here and there,
Now hasting and now gliding noiselessly,
I journey on past hill, and field, and town,
And lead my perfect life. All those who view
My passage love me. Birds stoop down and kiss
My lips and then rise up and sing. The sun
And stars shower benedictions. Children oft
Play near, and tune their laughter by my waves;
And men will let me journey through their land,
Nor call me trespasser, because they know
I drain their fields, and turn their many mills.
My life is ever happy, and all day
I follow on with faith and hope, and so
God leads me from the mountain to the sea.

Would'st thou be likewise happy? Then know
    this:
Thou hast a guide like that which guidest me,
Given thee in thy very earliest days,
To tell thee what is right and what is wrong,
And choose the central best, twixt good and better.
Thy Conscience is this guide, God's whisper-voice.
Oh, be as tender to its spirit touch
As weather vanes are to the summer winds,
Or flowers to dews of Heaven. Thus, by listen-
    ing,
Thou shalt plainer hear; and, by obedience,
Obeying shall grow easier; and thy life
Shall be a blessing to all sons of men.
So thy brief passage through this world shall be,
Not like the flight of some fear-blinded bird,
That strikes 'gainst trees and houses in its flight,
And shortly dies; but like my peaceful waves,
So shall thy days pass onward fearlessly,
Thy past a present pleasure, present days
All crowned with joy, and future days with hope.
Then when thou enterest the gloom of death,

Even as I approach this builded bridge,
Thou shalt discern how short the shadow is
That spans thy path, and thou shalt see beyond,
A vista brighter than the gates of morn,
Where thou may'st find thy destiny, and lead
A wider life through widening fields of change.

TO NATURE

The heart of Nature being everywhere music.—Carlyle.

DEAR Mother Nature! Sing to thee,
    Who hast so often sung to me?
Much rather would I choose to listen
Unto thy softest whispered word,
In murmuring leaves and waters heard,
Where sifting moonbeams glance and glisten,
Than mar the concord with my voice.
Alas, that I have but one choice,
For I am mured in city walls.
Imprisoned thus, my spirit calls
To thee of whom I only spy
The splendor of thy loving eye —
The solemn, sweet, protecting sky —
Still bending, tender as of yore.
And yet, a brighter look it wore
In days when on my native hills
I whistled away my boyish ills,
Merrily drove the kine afield,
Breathing the sweet perfume of dew,
While all my joyous nature knew
The blessings that May mornings yield!

Kind Mother Nature! I but send
A letter thus to thee, to say
That though in city streets I stray,
I love thee yet, my earliest friend;

For memory makes me even now
Feel thy cool kisses on my brow.
What time I leave the dusty streets,
I feel like one who, homeward bound,
Leaves boat or car, and, looking round,
The welcome of a dear face meets.
For even thus thy beauty greets
My hungry eyes, a welcome home;
While field, and stream, and forest dome
Break out in music, speech, and smiles
That lure me down the forest aisles
Where wandering winds their trumpets blow,
And make me worship ere I know.
Oh, take us when our hearts are wrong
And let us hear thy soothing song!
When our dull souls thy spirit spurn,
Like weather vanes that will not turn,
Set us up on a breezy hill;
There, counter-currents lost below,
To trim ourselves, and pointing, show
Our faces where God's winds do blow!

How I remember all thy dresses,
Fair Mother Nature! How thy tresses
Swing in the wind from forest trees,
And how thou wearest birds and bees
And flowers to suit each changing season —
Quaint ornaments that show thy reason,
When trailing emerald robes the hills,
The arbutus thy bosom fills;
In shimmering clouds of Summer drest,
A wild rose lies upon thy breast;
In Autumn's spangled red and gold,
Thy arms a load of apples hold;
Or when in snow thy beauty hides,
A snowbird on thy shoulder rides!

TO NATURE

Oh, well I love the somber grays
Thou wearest on the cloudy days!
Anon, when evening skies are bare,
The diamonds glitter in thy hair,
And, nestling in a cloud of lace,
Thy crescent pin shines in its place;
Then is thy step as blithe and gay
As maiden's on her bridal day!
Thus, ever varying, yet the same,
The years go by and leave thee young
But not thy children; we are stung
Soon to old age. Are we to blame?

Sweet Mother Nature! Right thou art,
Time draws no wrinkles on the heart.
Across the soul's serene expanse
More beauteous mornings yet may glance,
And merrier choirs in statelier trees
Freight with rare melody the breeze!
The sunrise gilds the robin's breast
Upon the maple's top at rest,
And lest I do the robin wrong,
I pause and listen for his song.

THE RECORD OF HAPPINESS

A KING, who languished in his bed,
    And wished to test his peoples' weal,
Called to his minister, and said:
  " Go, I my people's pulse would feel.

" In yonder square, the throng among,
  Hang a great book with pages white,
And let these words be o'er it hung;
  Let all whose lives are happy write."

All day came troops of curious folk
  And read the legend o'er the book.
Some smiled, some sighed, some lightly spoke,
  Some turned away with thoughtful look.

Old age came tottering on his staff,
  And youth with all the wealth of life,
The reveler paused and checked his laugh —
  'Twas passed by maiden, bride, and wife.

A doting mother held her child,
  And toying with the pen it tried
To write; the mother saw and smiled,
  But quick it dropped the pen and cried.

Just with the sun's last lingering look
  A beggar tottered to the stand.
They found — when couriers sought the book —
  The pen clasped in his lifeless hand.

When to the king the book was sent,
  He gazed on the unsullied page.
" None happy? I must be content."
  'Tis said he lived to good old age.

YE DUTCHE TOWNE GIRLES
(To the Belles of New York.)

WHAT burgh so poore it cannot boaste
    Of comely maids, a gentle hoste?
What hamlet ye have wandered bye
Was lit not by a damsel's eye?
And ye do welle, ye swains, to trye
    Their praises wide to winge;
        But saye no worde
        Till I be hearde,
    While Dutche Towne Girles I singe!

YE DUTCHE TOWNE GIRLES

Thysse Towne I singe lyes near ye shore
And holds two million soules or more;
   Yet it doth growe in such a waye
   Two million scarce would be astraye;
   Regarding whiche some folke do saye —
     And 'tis a harmlesse thinge —
        That thysse is due
        Largely to you —
   Ye Dutche Towne Girles I singe.

So waxes Dutche Towne more and more;
Each pretty maid attracts a score
   Of other folke, as ye knowe welle,
   The while they flocke from hille and delle,
   Here in a mighty clanne to dwelle
     And wide their edicts flinge;
        So greate the power
        Is at thysse houre
   Of Dutche Towne Girles I singe.

For they can dresse so brave and neate
From comely head to dainty feete,
   With proper snood or jaunty hatte,
   A bodice neither round nor flatte —
   And skirts that match like tit for tat —
     Could he but see them swinge,
        Old Peter Stuy —
        Vesant would eye
   These Dutche Towne Girles I singe!

And since their grandmammas were seene
On Battery Walle and Bowling Greene,
   With stately heads y' powdered welle,
   No other damsels may excelle
   Those whose fine grace I cannot telle
     As on Broadway in Springe,

> Like flowers a-rowe
> They gaily goe —
> Fair Dutche Towne Girles I singe!

Nor doe they all neglect ye minde
To culture welle, as ye will finde.
> With a sweet studiousness of lookes
> They often browse on goodlye bookes;
> They babble French like merry brookes,
>> Anon some sampler bringe
>>> That showes their parte
>>> In works of Arte —
> Wise Dutche Towne Girles I singe.

A racquet they can swinge so feate,
Or sit a prancing steede so fleete,
> That one would be a foole to saye
> It should be done another waye.
> And when their fingers lightly straye
>> Upon ye trembling stringe,
>>> They charme ye aire
>>> With musick rare —
> Sweet Dutche Towne Girles I singe!

Then gaily decked in Kirmesse stalle
Their glances holde my hearte in thralle,
> Or on ye coach-box seated highe
> Their beauty shines against ye skye,
> Or when ye fiddler's fingers flye —
>> Grouped in a merrye ringe,
>>> With slippered feete
>>> None dance so neate
> As Dutche Towne Girles I singe.

True that from these ye mighte not knowe
They cared for aughte but worldlye showe;
> Yet when ye Sabbath spreads its skies
> They bowe ye head with closed eyes;

And many mornings as I rise
I see them sweetly bring
Such goodlye loades
To poor abodes —
Kind Dutche Towne Girles I singe.

So, swains, I rede ye to beware
Our Dutche Towne Girles, and if ye care
For other maid with her abide,
And shield your hearte and eke your pride
From eyes that kille so farre and wide
Ye cloven-footed kinge
In terror flees
Whene'er he sees
Our Dutche Towne Girles I singe!

THE BEGGAR MAID

THE winds of the winter are keenest that blow
Round the bleak, brownstone walls of the millionaires' row.
And the sin of uncharity seems most unkind
In a street full of palaces swept by the wind.
Thus it was in the gloom of a December night
As two met on the avenue; one with her bright,
Ragged shawl drawn close round her face and her form,
And her skirts blown and torn, seemed a wraith of the storm!
The other was clad well from headpiece to toe,
And the lamp threw his long silhouette on the snow.

"Could you spare me a penny?" a pleading voice said.
But the man strode along without turning his head.

"Don't bother me, girl, you can work for your
 living."
And he said to himself: "I can't always be giv-
 ing!"
"But please, sir!" she cried, as she followed him
 close,
"You have a bouquet; would you give me a
 rose?"

At her touch Allan Gray at once slackened his
 pace,
And he thought, as he threw a sharp glance at
 her face,
That, somewhere, he had seen the girl's features
 before.
But then he had traveled two continents o'er,
Seen fair faces at courts, at beaches and balls,
And others, wine-flushed ones, in Revelry's halls.
So he only looked once at the bright, pleading
 eyes
And thought: "Hum! She's pretty, good figure
 and size!"
"No, girl! Are you crazy? Think you I've been
 buying,
At a dollar each, roses to keep you from crying?
Why, I carry the flowers to my own lady true:
Ha! To think they should go to a creature like
 you!
But you're saucy, I swear, and you're pretty as
 she,
But my flowers are my fortune with *her*, don't you
 see?"

A gust of wind near blew the shawl from her
 face,
Where a flush told how keenly she felt her dis-
 grace.

"Have a care, sir," she cried, " or your fair mistress may
Give you back your own roses to carry away.
There are places and times when flowers cease to be sweet,
And you'll want in the house what you slight in the street!"

Quick as flash down the side street the vision has flown,
And a laugh seems to float back to him there, alone.
Allan Gray had a practical turn to his mind,
And, of late, though his bachelor years had been kind,
He had said to his mirror: "Old man, you must marry,
You've more sins than a celibate safely may carry!"
Miss Edith Van Alstyne was comely and sweet,
Of good blood, and her father stood well on "the street":
And quoth Allan to Allan: "I'll charm this young dove,
She has beauty and money, I'll manage the love."

There are women whose hearts are as weak as their hands,
And who never withstand a *rich* suitor's demands;
Like the toys, which, if you give a coin to their hold,
Straightway open their doors and their treasures unfold!
There are others, thank God! like the bud of a rose,
That the sunshine of love will alone make unclose,

And no sweeter or truer of these ever grew
Than was Edith Van Alstyne, as shrewd people
   knew.

Ting-a-ling! went the bell at a stained crystal
   door,
While Allan breathed his roses' perfume o'er and
   o'er
Ere the summons was answered. "Miss Edith?
   Oh, yes;
She has just now come in, sah, and gone up to
   dress."
All parlors seem dreary when one has to wait,
So Allan scanned the paintings and gazed in the
   grate,
While he likened his heart to the fierce, glowing
   coal,
And a statue of Psyche to Edith, sweet soul!

Then came visions of nights at the opera flown,
When Wagner's sound-dreams or Bellini's sweet
   tone
Seemed to weave a new charm round a fair,
   thoughtful face
In box number nine. Ah, he well knew the
   place!
"I must push my scheme now," thought he.
   "Had I a lute,
Or that handsome new tenor to trumpet my suit!
I've spent enough money her coy heart to soften.
Yet, hang it! if she had accepted more often
The rides and the presents, and, yes, and my
   puns,
'Twould have suited me finely, despite florists'
   duns."

Anon, down the stairs swept a soft rustling dress,
Gleamed through the dark portières a draped loveliness,
And a voice, "Mr. Gray?" on the deep silence fell.
"Ah, how charming, Miss Edith, I hope you are well.
I brought you some roses. Those florists, the churls,
Begrudged me these beauties, the 'Mermets' and 'Pearls.'
Pray take them, and with them, for I cannot wait,
My love, and to-night, dear, oh, tell me my fate!"

Slowly raising her eyes from the floor as he closed,
With her form 'gainst the curtains unconsciously posed,
"Mr. Gray! Were I penniless, friendless, this hour,
Would you give me a penny, or even a flower?"
"Why, of course, I would give you my fortune, my all,
Now ask me for anything, I'll heed the call!"
"Then why, when I asked you a half hour ago,
Did you spurn me away? Does your heart vary so?
Yes, 'twas I, but don't think I was foolish to prove you,
To try if, unknown, unadorned, I could move you.
Had I begged of you love, still unheard might I go,
For I fear that you have none of that to bestow.
And, to-day, father's fortune is swept away quite,
So I play my true rôle as a beggar to-night.
What? 'That makes a *difference?*' Yes, so I thought.
Here, you are forgetting the roses you brought.

Why leave in such haste? You did never before!
And I thought you knew how to unfasten the
   door!
Let me help you. There, pull the small knob;
   here's your cane.
It's freezing — too bad — and beginning to rain!
Farewell! If you tell your friends father's sad
   tale,
Please mention his daughter is not yet for sale!"

Signora Piccova, in making her rounds,
Next morn clapped her hands and gave three
   little bounds,
As she found in an ash barrel, covered up warm,
Mr. Allan Gray's roses kept safely from harm,
And which, dusted and washed, made a nice little
   store
Of boutonnières to sell at an uptown club door;
While who should come sauntering slowly that
   way
And buy a pink rosebud but Mr. A. Gray!

Time had flown and had wafted in June's perfect
   weather,
When two men walked the avenue, talking to-
   gether.
The chimes of St. Thomas were ringing so gladly,
So tunefully, merrily, gayly, and madly,
That the twain stopped to see the gay people
   come out.
"Why! That's Miss Van Alstyne, without any
   doubt.
You know, Gray, her father went under last year,
But her ma had a million or two left, I hear."

Yes, the "beggar" is robed in rich satin and lace,
And the look of a happy bride softens her face,

"Hark to the voice of virgin forests sighing!
List to the hunter's cry upon the breeze!"
— *A Hymn to Ponus.*

While as Mendelssohn's music strikes on Allan's
    ears·
It carries a moral, for he fancies he hears:
A woman who's worthy to be a man's wife,
Though she has not a penny, is worth a man's
    life!

A HYMN TO PONUS
(Written for the dedication of the Monolith on Ponus Path, erected
by the New Canaan Historical Society.)

HARK to the voice of virgin forests sigh-
        ing!
    List to the hunter's cry upon the breeze!
Hark to the whisper of the arrow flying!
    Mark the struck deer quick bounding 'neath the
        trees!

Where is the Child of Nature, whose dim story
    We seek to reillume in modern rhyme?
Where are his haunts, the forests in their glory?
    The skies alone are left untouched by time.

Red, o'er the ridges where his footsteps wandered,
    Still gleams the orb he faced with filial eye;
Still shine the stars on which he nightly pondered
    In childlike wonder at their mystery.

To all our searching it is scarcely given
    To find of grave or wigwam any trace;
His paths are plowed, the very rocks are riven,
    Even the streams are tamed to lesser grace.

Breaking the clasp of Nature, his fond mother,
    Could he his eye upon this prospect range,
Sadly he'd say: Alas, my pale-face brother,
    He, the Great Spirit, only, does not change!

Change! Change is regnant always, yet, coeval,
  Resurgent Life beside him queenly reigns!
The blood that beat beneath the woods primeval
  Courses undaunted on in many veins.

And on the western prairies, bravely turning
  From the old ways to blaze their path anew.
In field and shop and school strong hearts are learning,
  And prove the red man's hand still deft and true.

White flocks and dappled herds his eye are filling
  With joy and pride as once the bear and deer;
Place for the hoe the tomahawk is willing,
  The corn-blade is the warrior's tasseled spear.

Full tardily our Ponus' name is graven
  On native rock to mark his burial spot.
What should we say if, to our duty craven,
  Our local sagamore should be forgot?

Here was his home. Down to the Sound's bright waters
  He fared, as we, when summer skies were blue.
There mingled, too, his dusky sons and daughters
  With those of Myanos and Wascussue.

His full-breathed lungs with purest breezes filling,
  Baring his rounded muscles in the chase,
His well-trained form to Nature's music thrilling,
  Healthful and unashamed he ran his race.

With mind too nobly framed for cheating others,
  To sordid greed of land at least no slave,

He sold for paltry coats to his white brothers,
  And hardly kept enough to hold his grave.
Then Nature called him, said: My child, no
    longer
  Essay to tend the maize or stalk the deer,
Nor bargain with thy brother who is stronger,
  But, nobly simple, sheathe the broken spear.

In days to come shall shine thy brave example,
  And men shall tell the pathos of thy race,
The proud dark owners of these acres ample,
  Who yielded up to fate with kingly grace.

Teach us the secret of such simple living,
  Teach us to face the sun and court the air,
To take the royal gifts of Nature's giving
  And envy not another's greater share.

Long may, on Ponus Path, this sentry standing,
  The sun, the stars, the hunter's moon, salute;
A silent figure, rugged and commanding,
  Bearing its message when our tongues are
    mute.

Yet, though we raise the stone and guard it duly,
  Stern Time, some day, shall bid the finger fall;
The only monument that serves us truly
  Is the heart's honest word, to each and all.

GREETING TO STAMFORD
      250th Anniversary (1641 — 1892).
  Read in the Town Hall, Stamford, Conn., Oct. 19, 1892.

THE fairest jewel on the sea's bright arm,
    Where southern slopes make wintry days
      seem warm,
Where on Long Island's bluffs one seems to see
Hints of the promised land that is to be,

THE CHORDS OF LIFE

Where mystic sails glide on the gentle swell,
And singing rivers aid the magic spell —
We greet thee, happy town, this natal morn —
A goddess rising from the sea, new born —
The Rippowam of times now passed away,
The fresh, bright, blushing Stamford of to-day!
As keeps America her festal year,
And proves four centuries have not made her sere,
How well may our fair city gaily laugh,
Whose age is but two centuries and a half!

What needs the eye that any tongue should tell
The wondrous changes that we see so well?
Since the first axe the forest woke from sleep,
And Ponus out of Progress' path did creep
(Selling the right of way so wondrous cheap);
Since Benton ruled with Puritanic sway,
Leading his flock in straight and narrow way,
Since Abram Davenport guided long and well
The fates and councils of this chosen dell,
And framed a tale for Whittier's pen to tell;
What wondrous wand has waved the region o'er,
Rolled back the virgin forest from the shore,
Bid stately homes and schools and churches stand
Where once the log-built cabin held the land,
And planted busy mill and teeming farm,
Protected by the Nation's mighty arm?
What now would fierce Miantonomoh say
To yonder warship, anchored in the bay?
No more may Toquam chief or Wascussue
Gaze on the Mataubaun they loved and knew;
No more the Indian maid's birch boat may glide
Where now the yachts in stately beauty ride;
And one must traverse many a ridge and dale
To strike to-day the vanished red man's trail.

GREETING TO STAMFORD

Not idly did the fathers choose for name
That of a spot long linked with England's fame,
Where Saxon Harold drave the northern foe,
By Derwent river, centuries ago.
For, since the sturdy Pilgrims planted here
Their first log cabins in a forest drear,
Moved by their mighty thirst for freer air,
Driven by bonds no Puritan could bear,
Its free-born title has not shown a flaw,
Nor known a conqueror save Peace and Law.
What though the prowling red man might assail,
And draw an Underhill upon his trail;
Though British guns might rake Ridgefield with fire,
Norwalk or Bedford glow, a patriot pyre;
And daring redcoats put to hasty flight
The gallant Putnam down the Greenwich height,
This spot has kept its " never-conquered " fame—
A green oasis in a prairie flame!

Is there a son of Stamford never knew
The ground where Tallmadge, Waterbury grew,
Nor guessed why — scorning any meaner glory —
His heart beat high at hearing Mather's story —
Dragged from his pulpit to the prison ships
To taste the last dread draught for patriot lips?
So, too, when Civil War overflowed its banks,
Drew one in ten to swell the loyal ranks,
How many knew the grief they could not speak
Save in the tear-drop on the mourner's cheek!
Look where a Hobbie's name shines with the rest.
Type of a love that yielded up its best —
A mother's offering to the deadly guns —
A new Niobe weeping for her sons!
Ah, speed the day when all this love we own
For that rare flower of chivalry now flown
Shall blossom in imperishable stone!

Peace to the Past! throughout the centuries dead
The Hand that led the Pilgrims still has led.
In their rude way they laid the bases broad
For liberty to live and worship God;
And sad for us if we shall yield a span
Of the great rights that make a man a man.

As rolling music, joyous faces greet
The wanderer in every festal street,
As the old town, with strong affection's arms,
Draws home her sons from seas and towns and farms,
We pledge her health with many an earnest prayer;
May taint of error ne'er pollute her air;
Still may the sea, the forest, and the field
Roll to her ample lap a fairer yield;
May every daughter, every stalwart son
Add to the fathers' work, so well begun,
That thus, fair Stamford, whosoever claim
Thy sisters pencil on the scroll of fame,
Thy sons need never blush to speak thy name!

"Seldom the stream is sought by human eyes,
This virgin beauty in its loveliness."
— *Peace Vale.*

LYRICS OF LIFE

PEACE VALE
(Rippowam River.)

THE cool arms of the hemlocks sway along
    The way that winds into the Vale of Peace,
Where piny odors, and the wood-bird's song,
    And low tree-murmurs hold perpetual lease. .

A vale of sorcery, the angler here
    Forgets the fishes, toying with his rod;
The painter, seated on the mossy weir,
    Over his palette soon will dream and nod.

Beneath the rude gray bridge is ever falling
    The fair young river, here in passion's foam;
And one may listen to the sea-nymphs, calling
    Their sister naiad from her mountain home.

Seldom the stream is sought by human eyes —
    This virgin beauty in her loveliness;
Only an old gray homestead, matronwise,
    Seems gravely looking at the river's stress.

But next the water takes a careless way,
    Singing and laughing as young maidens will,
Half startled where the gentle cattle stray,
    Or loitering, pensive, by the ruined mill.

Sometimes a veil of vapor intervenes,
    The trees are all a-glisten with its dew,
And there lie Nature's secrets, virgin scenes,
    And penetrable only to the few.

Last, like a bride, with half-concealèd smile,
    Pride in her bearing and her footstep free,
The river, 'neath a cool, green-fretted aisle,
    Moves, stately, to her wedding with the sea.

CHRISTMAS EMBLEMS
(The Star — The Yule-Log — The Holly — The Child)

BRIGHT heavenly guide that truly led
    The wise men from the east afar,
And paused above the manger-bed
    While angels smiled through doors ajar —
    Be thou our guiding star!

O Yule-log, weaving mystic gleams
    And shadows on the haunted floor,
Show us how through thy fervor streams
    The charity that, lit of yore,
    Glows kindlier evermore.

Amid the holly's glossy green,
    Or where the alder decks each bud,
The ruby berries, thickly seen,
    Shall typify that precious flood —
    His freely given blood.

And oh, sweet Child! the flower of love!
    Creation's crown! still gently win
Our hearts and souls to realms above,
    Afar from touch of soiling sin,
    Till we shall " enter in."

INSTRUMENTS

THE buffeted cliff by the main
    Drew the violin pine to its breast,
And soft was the wind-wakened strain
    Of the boughs by the breezes caressed,
Till a soul that had listened in pain
    Was lulled into infinite rest.

INSTRUMENTS

In a many-towered palace of state
   Stood a minstrel, all silvered with years.
Then his ruler, as cruel as great,
   Bade him sing for his prince and the peers;
And the heart that was hardened with hate
   Was melted to love and to tears!

A life that was simple and true
   Was chosen to meet a great need:
Through each rift of a duty to do
   Sprang a glory of sunburst — a deed —
Till he walked on a world that was new,
   And the sound of his name was a creed.

A FAREWELL TO YESTERDAY

WHERE is the road to Yesterday?
   Oh, tell in prose or rhyme;
For I would trace my backward way
   To that enchanting clime.

Life was so fresh and good and true,
   And friends so kind and fair.
Why should a day so bright and new
   All fade away in air?

Who knows the road to Yesterday?
   Is every seeker blind?
Say, does it cast no single ray
   To pilot those behind?

Oh, there's a road that leads our feet
   To hours more glad and bright;—
A road so short, a joy complete,
   A journey of a night!

Come, bid farewell to Yesterday!
   For in To-morrow's face
The happiest days now flown away
   Shine with a sweeter grace.

WHERE SHALL WE BURY HIM?

WHERE should we bury our dearest dead?
   Out in the meadow his grave should be,
Clover and daisies over his head
   Swaying and singing their psalmody;
For all the old world is sacred soil,
   And most the meadows, hallowed by toil.

Never a stone on his place of sleep,
But level the grass shall over him sweep;
Never the mower shall know if his feet
   Press his covering firmer down;
Nothing that molders, vain and fleet,
   Shall mock the gleam of his emerald crown.

We may not scatter our fading flowers
   Above his ashes with tender will;
But Spring, with hands more faithful than ours,
   Will bring the blossoms when ours are still;
Painting and building, above his breast,
Every season shall deck his rest.

So, year after year, the field will grow
A living pledge of the life laid low.
Nor would he ask for a fairer sign
   Than bobolinks, dipping and singing at morn,
Than careless straying of horses and kine,
   Than changing sentries of wheat and corn.

Why then cumber the sad, sweet world
   With moldering stone and crumbling urn,

Too weak to tell of the love impearled
   That flew to the city where jaspers burn?
Buried beneath this sea of grass,
God can find him when He doth pass.

THE BRIDGE

AT gallop, at gallop, through storm and night!
For over the river, with well-trimmed light,
   A woman her vigil doth keep.
She knows the torrent has burst its bounds,
The owl without makes boding sounds,—
   That into her heart do creep.

"O-ho-o-o! O-ho-o-o!" the white owl cries;
   "Your lover doth tarry long!"
Then saith the woman, as one more wise,
   "The bridge is safe and strong."

The rider has come to the river's brink,
He enters the bridge and little does think
   His fearful fate so near.
A crash, and a swirl, and he meets his death;
The waters have smothered his anguished breath,
   And the river flows dark and drear.

Still up by the cottage the white owl cries:
   "Your lover doth tarry long!"
And she, like one in a dream, replies:
   "The bridge is safe and strong."

What terrible sound is in the skies?
"The bridge, the bridge," she wildly cries.
   (There's rest on the cottage floor).
All night in the doorway the rain doth dash,
The owl is stricken by lightning flash,
   The river doth rage and roar;

While the wind goes by with a voice that saith :
   "The waiting is never long.
From the land of life to the land of death
   The bridge is sure and strong."

GERARDIA

PURE little bells, low swinging
      Along the pasture ways,
Accept my rustic singing
   Although I lack the bays !
For when the dew is ringing
   Your pink with diamond rays
There's nothing fairer springing
   In rich September days !

Like shy, sweet little lasses,
   Your faces, fresh and clear,
Salute one as he passes
   With courtesies kind and dear.
How glad I leave the masses
   To linger with you here !
Oh, greet me 'mong the grasses
   Till life is late and sere.

"HEIMGANG"

AS we go forth each hopeful, beckoning day
      To join in mirth or sterner lessons learn,
Most glad of all we find the homeward way
      And sweet return.

Thus, when life's day of work and play is past,
   And we no more with weary footsteps roam,
Sweetest of all will be to us at last
      The going home.

THE VOYAGE

THE music echoes along the shores,
   The barge goes gaily by;
It sails a river that never was known,
   And no man knoweth why.

And some of the voyagers forward gaze,
   Whose hearts with hope yet burn,
While others watch the waves behind
   And wish they might return.

THE RETURN OF THE SHIP

WITH banners her masts adorning,
   And fair as the ocean's foam,
The ship sailed out in the morning,
   Out of her harbor home.
All new from the hand of her maker,
   Who watched her sailing away
To battle with storm and breaker,
   To wrestle with wind and spray.

'Tis many a month since the sailing,
   But the builder is hopeful still;
As the glow in the west is paling,
   He stands on the seaward hill.
And the ship comes homeward slowly,
   All battered, and rent, and frayed;
But he welcomes her though she is lowly,
   For he loveth the ship he made.

O Builder of human vessels,
   That sail in the morning of youth
Out on the unknown ocean
   With yearning for light and truth!

Art Thou for Thy vessels watching,
   Awake on Thy seaward hill?
Wilt know us when, worn and weary,
   We wait for Thy further will?

CREEDS

ACROSS the bay the beacon shines
   To boatmen three, and sheds its light
Along the waves in glimmering lines
   To guide them through the night.

The great clouds darken, and the gale
   Dashes the spray with deafening roar,
As each to each the boatmen hail
   While toiling for the shore.

"The lighthouse lamp doth light for me
   A royal journey home;
Only to me, the path I see
   Gilding the crests of foam!"

"Nay, nay," the second says, "you boast,
   For straight from yonder headland bold,
Full on my boat, from off the coast,
   Flashes the line of gold!"

"The bay is black, both left and right,"
   Then laughs the last one of the three,
"But spirits bright have swept with light
   The path that leads to me!"

Ah, silly seamen, who, each day,
   Voyaging on the unknown sea,
Quarrel among yourselves and say,
   "The path leads but to me."

Could you change vessels, then for aye
   Would vanish selfish creed and whim,
Seeing how Love lights each a way
   To lead us home to Him!

THE OVER-CURTAIN

GALLERIES of art are thronged,
   Yet this Painter still is wronged!
Many prize the pictures framed,
Catalogued and aptly named —
Praising all the mimic skies,—
But, outdoors they have no eyes!
Here is faultless painting truly,
Girt by hills that frame it duly;
Here is art that charms the eye—
Glorious, ever-changing sky.
And the painting has this in it,
'Tis a new one every minute;
And one never tires of gazing,
Be it clear or softly hazing;
Be it bright, or gray and hoary,
Or a burst of sunset glory.
Never in the days of yore
Was it just like this before!
Ne'er again in sun or rain,
Will it be the same again!
Peasant, look! Your painting beats
The rarest one in London's streets!
Sight on land goes little way —
Through the sky it goes for aye;
Through the blue eternal miles
Still the wondrous vista smiles.
And it seems, sometimes, for certain
Heaven's beautiful drop-curtain,

Made to charm us till it raises
On the scene the Psalmist praises!

CITY PARKS

HOW I love the little spaces —
   Never failing founts of health —
Nature's beautiful oases
   In the desert sands of wealth!

Here the plashing fountains springing
   Shine like jewel-burdened sheaves;
To their cadence birds are singing
   Madrigals among the leaves.

Pansies in their lowly places,
   Spreading perfume through the grass,
With their sweet, unwrinkled faces,
   Seem to chide us as we pass.

Ah, poor children of the city,
   Who have never Nature known,
What a pity, what a pity,
   This is all of her you own.

Yet this glimpse unto you given,
   Source of courage yet may be,
Like the dreams we dream of Heaven,
   Knowing not what it shall be.

TO L. E. S. AND E. B. S.
(With "Wayside Music.")

GOOD *Shipmen*, by this murmuring stream —
   All storms forgot in summer's dream —
Pray take my "music by the way,"
As free as song from maple spray;

TO L. E. S. AND E. B. S.

Yet wishing it may ne'er intrude
Upon your bosky solitude;
Or if 'tis read while purrs the fall,
May seem an echo to its call —
So true to life, in some small jot —
Or in stream-music be forgot!

BIRDS OF PASSAGE

LIKE birds that southward fly
   When nights are growing long,
Looping across the evening sky
   A silver thread of song;

I hear the spirit wings
   Hastening over my head,
And my soul awakes and sings
   To the music they have shed.

And though my eyes are wet
   To see them fade in sky,
I think I hear their music yet,—
   Echoes that will not die.

And in the endless Springs,
   When Hope's fair blossoms burn,
Shall I not hear again their wings?
   Shall they not all return?

THE POET

I AM not young, I am not old,
   For Time has fled before me;
All gates before my touch unfold,
   Transparent skies are o'er me.

I gaze in maiden's eyes, and ken
  Their never-uttered speech;
I look into the souls of men
  Deeper than they can reach.

The sun each morn I link anew
  Unto my kingly cars;
Each evening drive through realms of blue
  My silver-harnessed stars.

My spirit speaks, and birds and bees
  Obey my slightest will;
And silent things break out in speech,
  And noisy things are still.

No noble thing escapes my love,
  All maidens pure are mine,
And ever round me, from above,
  The rays of beauty shine.

ON FORT GREENE, BROOKLYN

I LOVE to stand upon a hill;
  I know not why 'tis dearer,
Unless, childlike, I fancy here
  That heaven's a little nearer.

And so I linger here to-night,
  Down looking on the city,
Whose soft-ascending murmur fills
  My heart with awe and pity.

The weary thousands homeward go;
  It fairly makes me dizzy
To think that in each moving form
  A heart and brain are busy!

ON FORT GREENE, BROOKLYN

Oh, what a wondrous flood of men!
    What weariness and weeping
To have one glorious glance at life
    And then the unknown sleeping!

For who can help to question: Why?
    And: Whither are we tending?
To send the query to the sky
    And ask what is the ending?

The stars are wise, they will not speak,
    Yet hopefully keep shining;
Shall I not, too, do well to wait
    And watch without repining?

A glad boy whistles in the street,
    The merry car bells jingle,
The gun booms o'er the bay: "All's well!"
    Again my warm veins tingle.

Two lovers laugh and pass and then
    The dusk around them closes,
While from a bush below the wall
    I catch the breath of roses.

So, after all, what though we die
    If still the sky is blue?
If roses still are fair and sweet,
    And love is pure and true?

WHEN THIS SHALL BE DREAM

SOME say that we hope for our Heaven in vain,
The dream will prove false, not a shadow remain.
And yet I keep hoping a time may come, too,
When Earth shall be dream and Heaven be true.

We talk very wise as we play with Time's toys.
Ah, Father, forgive us, poor ignorant boys!
Believing in nothing unfelt or unseen,
With wonders all round of which we little ween.

Sometimes, tired of toiling, we bind up our wounds,
Grow weary of muck-rakes, and sick of earth's sounds,
And gaze where the stars in the blue heavens glow,
And say, Shall we ever from there look below?

O Earth, thou art fair, but thou art not complete,
I have dreamed of a country more beautiful, sweet;
And cannot help thinking of how it will feel
When this shall be dream and that shall be real.

TO-MORROW

THE little child goes out to play,
    With hope and happy thoughts he goes;
But disappointments cross the way,—
    He finds the thorn beneath the rose.
And tired at night to bed he goes,
    And dreams 'twill be a brighter day
        To-morrow.

The youth goes out to seek his fate,
    Through rural roads or crowded streets;
His hope is high, his soul elate,
    He counts as friends all whom he meets.
Alas, too soon the fancy fleets,
    Yet still he says, " I will be great
        To-morrow."

Grown to a man, in daily strife
    With brother men for daily bread,

Reality's too cruel knife
   Cuts all his youthful visions dead;
And night oft hears these sad words said,—
   " O God, I'll live a better life
        To-morrow."

In gray old age the golden gleam
   Still hangs around the fleeting guest;
And, standing just across the stream,
   The vision still invites his quest,
As, sinking to his final rest,
   He whispers in his dying dream,
        To-morrow.

Bright Day of Hope that ever holds
   Our earthly joys just out of reach,
And in thy happy hours enfolds
   Our dearest deeds and noblest speech;
Oh, drop one flying word, to teach
   That life to-day forever molds
        To-morrow.

THE COMING POET
(A Fragment.)

AH, the chords that only slumber
   Ready for his hand,
And the armies without number
   Waiting his command,
When the tramp of Truth's own legions
Shall o'erthrow the wrongs that cumber
   This predestined land;
Pæans following the victors,
   Wild and sweet and grand!

Then a rhyme shall still a cannon,
    And a stanza win a fight,
And a song shall rout a war cloud
    As the morning drives the night.
And the " doleful miserere,"
    Played upon the iron keys,
Shall give way to chants of gladness
    And the overture of peace.

And the theme that's ever new,
Love of man and maiden true,
Shall make eyes of women glisten
With such songs as one might listen
    To in starry spheres;
While the blood that swiftly rushes
Shall bloom out in happy blushes,
    Or distil in tears.

So shall speed the happy years,
    The harvest days of Time;
So the bard, in radiant tiers,
    Shall build the walls of rhyme;
And ring the music of the spheres
    As on a heavenly chime.

ARGONAUTS

WE come from far, forgotten shores
    In sailless ships, o'er soundless seas;
We search the world for precious ores
    And life's rich golden fleece.

We treasure the shining grains of truth,
    Treasure the smile and kindly deed,
Treasure the brightness of early youth,
    And soon to our homes we speed.

We speed to spend our spirit wealth
   In the light of a better day;
The sands of time we leave behind,
   But the gold we carry away.

TO JAMES WHITCOMB RILEY

SINGING and whistling on his woodland way,
   We thought we heard a happy, careless boy
   Filling the forest with a sound of joy
As leafy aisles prolonged each early lay.
The rustling of the silken ranks of corn,
   The cry of swimmers in the shady pool,
   Sweet, moonlight trysts in evenings calm and cool,
And orchard fragrance on his songs were borne.

Now, in the open glade, take your own place
   That waits beneath the greenwood tree of song!
   Welcome from those who did not judge you wrong,
But said "A singer," ere they saw his face.
Take up your reed and charm us once again!
   Happy the land where minstrel notes repeat
   In newer measures, wild and fresh and sweet,
The simple themes whose beauty cannot wane.

The scenes of toil, the restful hours of peace,
   The cabin idyls, prairie gloom and glow,
   Make lilt and sing till all the folk shall know
And tell them to the children at their knees!
Aye, pipe and sing each new surprising lay,
   And plaudits new if with a greater joy
   You fill the ears you pleased when, like a boy,
You sang and whistled on your woodland way!

TO A MOUSE AT A BALL

YOU timid little quadruped!
    Why do you shake your glossy head,
    And blink in sore affright,
Like children that fall out of bed
    In middle of the night?

Nay, does it fill your heart with shame
To wear this soft, gray dress, the same
    You wore perhaps last year?
Yet you can rank yon jeweled dame
    In modesty, my dear.

What! Have you no gay cavalier
To whisper flattery in your ear,
    Bird, toad, or cricket?
Then tell, how did you get in here
    Without a ticket?

But now I must be in a dream,
You're one of Cinderella's team
    So cute and chipper!
Tell me, how can I catch a gleam
    Of that glass slipper?

Mousie, like me, you love the best
Your own soft, cosy little nest,
    Far from this bustle,
Whose "charity" seems half suppressed
    By silken rustle.

But see yon giant with a broom!
Intent upon your awful doom
    An usher comes!
Quick! Creep into the supper room
    And get some crumbs.

Yet 'tis the " shining share " of Burns
A little " beastie " safely turns
   From threatened ill!
Thanks to the plowman bard who earns
   Our own good-will!

THE CYCLE

THIS is the toy, beyond Aladdin's dreaming,
   The magic wheel upon whose hub is wound
All roads, although they reach the world around,
O'er western plain or Orient desert gleaming.

This is the skein from which each day unravels
   Such new delights, such witching flights, such joys
   Of bounding blood, of glad escape from noise,
And ventures beggaring old Crusoe's travels!

It is as if some mighty necromancer,
   At king's command, to meet a lady's whim,
   Instilled such virtue in a rubber rim
And brought it forth as his triumphant answer.

For whereso'er its shining spokes are fleeting,
   Fair benefits spring upward from its tread,
   And eyes grow bright, and cheeks all rosy red,
Responsive to the heart's ecstatic beating.

Thus Youth and Age, alike in healthful feeling,
   And man and maid, who find their paths are one,
   Crown this rare product of our century's run
And sing the praise, the joy, the grace of wheeling.

CROSSING EAST RIVER BRIDGE

NIGHT'S darkest curtains hang around;
    Yon bridge, a wondrous web of wires,
Spans the bent arm 'twixt sea and Sound —
    Twin cities burn their beacon fires.

The long arc of electric light,
    With steady and far-reaching rays,
Shadows upon the waters bright
    The structure's cables, ropes, and stays.

Godlike its majesty and rest,—
    Mute challenge to the centuries' roll, —
But ever runs in fruitless quest
    The river, like a human soul.

QUATRAINS

A CHARACTER

ONCE a fire-shaken Mount of Pain,
    Now, passion-quenched, it meekly holds
A cool, deep cup to keep God's rain —
    Blessed by the burden it enfolds.

ADVERSITY

A fine, hard face has sovereign Fate
Which frowns us on to higher ends;
Transfigured, how it makes amends
When Love smiles through the mask of Hate!

REQUIREMENTS

He loves a woman little who
    Sees not an angel in her,
And will not hate his dearest sin
    And conquer it to win her.

QUATRAINS

TRUTH

Truth is a strong and widening stream
   That floweth evermore;
And knowledge but the nearer waves
   That break upon the shore.

TO RHYMERS

Be sure your song is from the heart,
Not every theme is worth your art;
Seems then your subject worthy still?
Then give it naught but finest skill!

UTTERANCE

There is a Word, that, spoken, flies
Echoless ever through the skies;
Its Utterance, full, takes all life's breath;
The monosyllable of Death.

CONCORD
(To L. M. Alcott.)

I WENT to see the Poet in his home
   Where Concord guards its genius-memoried
         plain,
Royally round its meadows I did roam,
   For troops of visions formed a kingly train.

And yet I did not touch his honored hand,
   Nor did I gaze into those eyes so wise;
For thus I thought: Have I not met his mind?
   'Tis better than the "meeting of the eyes."

Stay in thy station like the steadfast stars,
   Or sunlit summits of the mountains hoary;
Too near approach the finer music mars,
   Ye lose the brightness, and ye lose the glory!

The gold of friendship overweighs the dross
   Of fame, and so a willing way I wend
With her, the good, and count it not a loss
   To leave the Poet and to love the Friend.

THOMAS CARLYLE
(Died Feb. 5, 1881.)

GONE, the Hero-worshipper,
   To the land where heroes live!
One more star is in the heavens,
   And one less has earth to give.

"He has lived his life," men say,
   Yet his spirit knows not age;
Skyward longing, it has burst,
   Like an eagle, from its cage!

No more mighty blows of Thought,
   Roughly worded, tender-hearted!
Ah, that scholars knew their love
   Ere the Teacher had departed!

Poet, too, who saw more beauty
   Than his critics ever rhymed!
They, like beasts the farmer feedeth,
   Shook the ladder which he climbed!

Mourn him not in lines dolorous,
   He needs not a single tear:
In the place we dream of, o'er us,
   He is more at home than here.

Goethe, Dante there will meet him,
    And his own melodious brother,
Robert Burns, who waits to greet him,
    Worthy son of Scotland Mother!

Royal spirit, take thy rest!
    Thou art richer, we are poorer;
Yet because thou hast been with us
    Life is manlier, Heaven surer.

REQUIEM
(Josiah Gilbert Holland.)

THE sun climbs up the eastern sky,
    And sinks as surely in the west;
No prophet now may bid it stand
    Until it reach its destined rest;
Nor may our prayers or tears prolong
    The lives of those we love the best.

The noisy followers of Fame —
    Surely enough of these are sent.
Too few such kindly men as he,
    Whose actions matched his good intent;
Whose life is its own eulogy,
    His memory his monument.

To crown a brave, pure, Christian life,
    Is Heaven itself a meed too high?
Will He, who showers His gifts on earth,
    To such as him we mourn, deny
A fairer home among the stars,
    The Thousand Islands of the sky?

IN MEMORIAM

(K. V. F. C.)

NOT to grow old — it was her oft-told hope,—
   And when at rest not to be thought as lying
There in the ground, upon the grassy slope,
   But watching near us with a love undying;
A gentle presence, haunting us to bless,
And soothe our loneliness.

To live, to work, to hope, to greet each day
   With cheerful welcome for its lowliest duty,
To suffer patiently the hurts that slay,
   To make a life of toil a path of beauty,—
This was the lesson she was wont to trace
Before the proud world's face.

And, for reward, it was enough to meet
   A baby's welcome from the daily task;
Love from a few could make the bitter sweet,
   Pity from none the brave, proud heart would ask;
And with the burden of the longest mile
Could carry, too, a smile.

A face from which the deepest grief would flee
   At loving words, or looks of love unspoken,—
It seems to say: Now let that love for me
   Bear its full test, and grief by love be broken;
For Sorrow's fullest blessing ne'er appears
Till Sorrow wipes its tears.

Peace to the snow-white hands that would not rest
   Till greater Love had bid their duties cease;

IN MEMORIAM

Peace to the fearless sentry in her breast —
    To sunny spirit, gentle footsteps, peace!
Echo of storms or words of worldly strife,
Mar not her newer life.

So, as the trees, still shuddering in the gale,
    Tremble with song while yet the raindrops fall;
Or as the violet lifts its features pale,
    Knowing which way the heavenly forces call;
We fare, as travelers, when the storm is by —
Our sun is in the sky.

SPRING SONG
(Suggested by Mendelssohn.)

I.

WHAT makes you sing so gladly?
    What makes you sing so madly?
Because the Spring is coming,
Because the Spring is near;
When sweetest flowers are blowing,
And merry brooks are flowing,
And every lad is going
    To meet the lass that's dear!
It's all because it's Springtime,
It's all because it's Springtime,
    Merry, merry Springtime,
    Merry, merry Spring!

II.

What makes you laugh so lightly?
What makes you smile so brightly?
    Because the Spring is coming,
    Because the Spring is here!
Heigho, the birds are wooing,
The snowy doves are cooing,
And rosy lads undoing
    The hearts that are so dear!
It's all because it's Springtime,
It's all because it's Springtime,
    Merry, merry Springtime,
    Merry, merry Spring!

"SWEETHEART, BE TRUE"

SWEETHEART, be true, what though I stray
    From Love's divine, appointed way,

Still keep thy lofty heavenly track,
To guide thy wandering sailor back ;
Clear shining in the depths of blue,
Sweetheart, be true !

Sweetheart, be true, though sundered wide
By forest, plain, or rolling tide !
Love's sun shall gild for each the day,
And guide each love-thought all the way.
Though longing eyes the miles may rue,
Sweetheart, be true !

Sweetheart, be true. When God's own light
Shall drive away the night of night,
Meet me with dewy, tender eyes —
So meet to habit Paradise —
Where love at last shall have his due !
Sweetheart, be true !

OH, LOOK FROM OUT THE STARRY SKIES

(Song.)

THE stars are gleaming far and bright ;
    The winds are keen and cold ;
The woolly flocks, all snowy white,
    Are cuddling in the fold.
But in my heart such longing lies —
    Bright star of yonder shore !
Oh, look from out the shining skies
    And hear me as of yore !

The world is wrapped in slumber deep,
    All other hearts at rest,
While mine, too aching full for sleep,
    Keeps up its lonely quest.

And still my prayers in ardor rise
   And climb up more and more —
Oh, bend from out the starry skies
   And kiss me as of yore!

Oh, what has Love to do with years,
   Or Death to do with Love!
Can Time o'er-rule a lover's tears
   Or dim those stars above?
Still, still, up to yon Paradise
   My song should nightly soar —
Oh, fly from out those lovely skies
   And love me as of yore!

AN OLD-FASHIONED SONG

THE months may come, the months may go,
   The frosty winds come leaping,
And silent 'neath the driven snow
   The hearts of flowers be sleeping.
There lives yet in each soothèd vein
   The dauntless will to blossom
When pink arbutus crowns again
   The hills of earth's fair bosom.

So in my true love's gentle heart,
   Though forces dire be waging
To draw me from that breast apart,
   Her constant watch engaging,
I know that where Love plants his seed
   'Twill grow to sweet fruition,
And buds of thought and flowers of deed
   Fulfil their tender mission.

Oh, never yet a sun went down
   But came again in splendor!

Oh, never yet Love tried to frown,
  But cast a side glance tender!
While joyfully I sing my part
  In our sweet song undying,
There blends the music of her heart,
  With love to love replying.

A MEADOW SERENADE
(Tune, " Bonnie Sweet Bessie.")

IF I were a gay caballero,
  And you were a fair Spanish maid,
I would doff you my plumèd sombrero
  And sing you my best serenade.

CHORUS.
  Hay time, play time,
  The sweet of the year is for you and me.

I would sing of your eyes in their brightness,
  Of the lashes so long and so brown,
I would sing of your neck in its whiteness,
  Your footstep so light and so strong.

Your voice in its freshness and sweetness,
  The smile rippling over your face,
All the charm of your maiden completeness
  Would find in my ballad a place.

But alas for sweet Fancy's armada,
  And the dream-ships so fair and unreal,
For I am no son of Granada,
  And you are no maid of Castile!

Yet to thee, my fair fellow-haymaker,
  I would bring back the glad summer time,
With its charm of the pitcher and raker,
  And weave all in sweet-scented rhyme!

THE CHORDS OF LIFE

Here's a song for those innocent blisses
　　When we cared not a fig for good form,
When we threw clover blossoms for kisses,
　　And captured the haycocks by storm!

So give me my straw hat for sombrero,
　　And with you in a green meadow glade,
And I'll envy no gay caballero,
　　Nor sigh for a fair Spanish maid.

A SEA SONG

SWEET, for the quest of thee —
　　Sweet, for the test of thee —
Bright shines the moon on the rim of the sea,
While I am gliding on,
Striding on, riding on,
　　Mad with the thirst that your lips gave to me.

Though hearts be quivering,
Though ships be shivering,
　　Night and its demons break out of their grave,
Swift to my Beautiful,
Draw me, love dutiful,
　　Love, like a storm-bird that laughs at the wave.

Sick of the motion-dirge,
Of the wide ocean-surge,
　　Brackish the waves of life, naught I may drink,
Only where, swelling up,
Sweet waters, welling up,
　　Mark me my fountain, your dear lips the brink.

WHEN LOVE DOTH LIE A-DREAMING
(A Song.)

WHEN Love doth lie a-dreaming
   His weapons you may spy —
His arrows by him gleaming,
   And eke his bow doth lie.

But when he is assailing
   Some maiden's tender heart,
It is all unavailing
   To think to see his dart.

His bunch of fatal lances,
   And eke his mighty bow,
Display but in his glances,
   Or in his smile do show.

Who'd think that eyes so pleading
   Had ever, mocking, laughed?
Or his red lips, receding,
   Could speed such fatal shaft?

O maids, who hope to capture
   His arms of sorcery,
Seek him when noonday rapture
   A-dreaming makes him lie!

Thus, when the sun is beaming,
   Go steal his arms away;
For when thou art a-dreaming
   Then Love will have his day!

HEART TO HEART

HEART, seek her heart who dwells apart,
   And plead to be her guest,
That in her grace she grant you place
   To lie upon her breast.

There, 'twixt those hills where sweetly thrills
  The current of her life,
In fragrant rhyme, forget all time,
  All fear, or pain, or strife.

Nor lightly prize light from her eyes,
  Her smiles that sweetly bless,
If fingers soft should touch thee oft,
  Or her red lips caress.

But oh, mark this, to never miss
  The tale her heart doth tell;
That doth repeat in every beat
  How she doth love me well.

So, heart of gold, thy quest unfold —
  As I thy course have sped;
Nor backward speed unless, indeed,
  She wants my heart instead.

ANGEL HEART

ANGEL heart and woman form!
    All my praise thou art above;
Thou hast cleared my life of storm
  With the sunshine of thy love.

Let me love thee my life long,
  Then in heaven renew my song,
When thy day of death shall part
  Woman form and angel heart!

WITH LILACS

I BEG the pardon of these flowers
    For bringing them to one whose hair
Alone doth shame, beyond compare,
  The sweetest blooms of richest bowers.

I beg the pardon of this maid
For offering them with hand less pure,
A heart less perfect, needing cure
By Love's own music, softly played.

CAPITULATION

OVERLOOKING my dominions,
    Seeming near yet seeming far,
Stood a proud and stately castle,
    Ever challenging to war.

Beautiful were its surroundings,
    Many a winding way was there,
Many gayly flaunting banners
    Fluttered in the golden air.

So I came to storm the castle,
    And with many a cunning art
Through its windows or its gateway
    Shot my arrows at its heart!

Then down fell the airy stronghold —
    Perished in a mist away;
Out there stepped a lovely maiden,
    And she loved me from that day.

She is free from her enchantment,
    Pledged to love who set her free;
So, in place of haughty castle,
    Smiles a loving face at me!

COLUMBIA
(A National Song.)

PURE as the air that blows across
    Thy many mountains old;
Warm as the fire that drives the dross
    Off from the shining gold;

Bright as the stars that watch above
  Thy prairies broad unrolled ;
True as the truest tale of love
  That e'er was sung or told ;
    Is the love we bear to thee,
    O Queen of the Land and Sea !
    Columbia ! Columbia !
    Thou Home of Liberty !

Long as we love the sacred ties
  That love has given birth ;
Long as we love the memories
  That twine around each hearth ;
Long as our best life-blood to thee
  Shall be of any worth ;
Long as we hope our heaven shall be
  When we shall leave the earth ;
    Will we pray and fight for thee,
    Will we live and die for thee ;
    Columbia ! Columbia !
    Thou Home of Liberty !

A DESIRE

DAUGHTER of Dawn and of Twilight,
  Spirit of calm and delay,
Hater of haste and of high-light,
  Nurse of the slow, dying day : —
Bring me thy peace-giving potion —
  Essence of mountain and sea —
Give me thy lips for a lotion ;
  Come — come to me — come to me !

Others will sing thee more sweetly,
  Others will courtlier bow ;
Others will toast thee more neatly —
  Bringing the blush to thy brow.

A DESIRE

Ah, but my longing is tragical,
   Holding my breath till I feel
Touch of thy finger-tips magical
   Over my temple-pulse steal.

Yes, I was sure of thy presence —
   Love is the magical rose!
Light as the whirr of the pheasants
   Hastens my maiden — Repose!
Daughter of Dawn and of Twilight,
   Spirit of calm and delay,
Hater of haste and of high-light,
   Nurse of the slow, dying day.

HER LITTLE FOOT
(Rondeau.)

HER little foot, exposed to view,
   As on the wall she sits askew,
Beneath her petticoat doth show
Like April bud in bank of snow,
So shy, yet daring to peep through.

I wot that,— though I never knew
The dainty links between the two —
   Yet from her winsome face I'd know
      Her little foot!

She sketches clouds, and depths of blue,
And trees, and birds of dapper hue,
   The while I watch swing to and fro
   That foot. like fairy rocking slow,
Till, drawn by it, I draw it, too —
      Her little foot.

FOUR GUARDSMEN

THERE are four little letters that live in my
    heart —
  An L, and an O, and a V, and an E,
And at sound of your name those letters will
    start
  And form into line like a drilled company!

They are brave little warriors, faithful and true,
  Four guardsmen, as leal as were e'er known to
    fame;
Their captain is L, and I need not tell you
  How they spring into line at the sound of your
    name.

My heart is their fortress, and every day
  It echoes with melody, martial and sweet;
At the sound of your name their bugles will play,
  And I hark for the sound of their hurrying
    feet.

At the sound of your name they delight to hold
    fast
  My heart 'gainst all comers, whoever they be;
They will keep its green ramparts 'til life is o'er-
    past —
  My four good defenders — L, O, V, and E.

THE TRYST

SWEET Lady, I have watched thee now for
    years,
  Taking thy stand beneath the almond tree;
When twilight fades, when the shy moon out-peers,
  And stars steal out, then also cometh thee.

THE TRYST

Yes, we are chosen friends, the stars and me;
They are so patient, and they watch so late;
   They may have lovers, too. Howe'er that be,
True love can wait.

But time is fleeting, like the silver light,
   The fickle light, that leaves the river's breast;
The winds are robbing blossoms of their white,—
   And ah, how lonely is an empty nest!
      Yet time and light and bloom touch not my quest;
I could not leave, unguarded, to its fate
   My rose of faith for all the world holds best.
True love can wait.

Perhaps thy lover ill deserves thy trust.
   What if another claims his wayward heart?
Then if he treads thy passion in the dust,
   Choose some one else, and gayly play thy part!
      Ah no, for love with me is not an art!
Nor would I curse my lover in such state;
   False lights may tempt my sailor from his chart—
True love can wait.

Still thou art sinful — wasting strength and youth.
   Forgetting woman's duty, all thy friends;
Loving a shade, some other's love, forsooth!
   Come, drop thy vigil, fate will make amends.
      I will not slight my duty nor life's ends;
My chief love makes my other loves more great;
   Can Love be loved too much? That me defends!
True love can wait.

Sweet Lady! Let me seek thy dearest out;
   Such love as thine the whole dull world must
      leaven.
Make me thy messenger, and have no doubt!
   How may I know him? Hast thou tokens given?

*Yes, we were pledged when sunset skies were
    riven,*
With gifts of roses, by this wood-path gate.
  *Till night, till morn, till age, till death, till
    heaven,*
True love can wait.

O Love! My boat is rocking on the tide,
  I know the light that flashed between our eyes
So long ago, here by the river-side!
  Oh, dost thou know me, Love, my bride, my
    prize?
  O Love, if I had dreamed such dear surmise
My kisses would have made my tongue abate!
  Oh, write it on the gates of Paradise: —
True love can wait.

MY RIDDLE

> Who telleth me one of my meanings
> Is master of all I am. —*Emerson.*

THE sphinx must needs surrender
    When its riddle was guessed away;
  Could I have been less tender,
    When mine was guessed one day?

  That day I built and decked with bloom,
    And ever so dainty art,
  A snowy shrine in a little room
    In the house I call my heart.

  Often a little girl enters there,
    Her face each day I see;
  But no one else the door must dare,
    She, only, has the key.

And yet 'tis an illusion,
  Like the lake in the desert sand.
God only knows how the world may use
  The girl I thought so grand.

The veil of the future I cannot part,
  Yet something makes me trust
That after this house I call my heart
  Has crumbled away to dust,

When the world no more may draw her,
  When its mask has passed away,
I shall know her as I saw her
  On that one sweet, summer day.

A GIFT TOO GRAND

WHAT though I think, my thoughts of thee
    Find nothing with thee to compare.
Can Beauty's fairer sister be
    By Beauty's garments made more fair?
In dreams I see the rose-crowned hills
    That hide in silvery clouds of lace,
While through and through and through me thrills
    The gentle influence of thy face;
The loving lips so quick to ope —
    True sentinels each pearly tooth —
The forehead like a hill of hope —
    The eyes beneath, like springs of truth!
Wild storm and wind may rack the skies,
    And rolling thunder vex the air,
They cast no shadow on thy eyes —
    I gaze in them — the day is fair!
What though another's ships have sped
    To search the East for spices rare?
I will but bend above thy head
    And catch the perfume of thy hair.

So doth thy precious beauty soar,
    A temple white and free from wrong,
Whose years but make it, more and more,
    So like a flower, so like a song.
And thou art mine, a gift too grand,
    As if a shepherd, proud but poor,
Should woo and win a princess' hand,
    Or beggar find a Kohinoor.

SANCTUARY

O LOVE, is this thy own dear land,
    And thine the silvery hours?
Then knight me with thy own fair hand —
    An accolade of flowers!

Now lucent eyes and happy face —
    The stars are in thy train;
The lilies blush in their disgrace,
    The rose resigns her reign!

When on that temple's domes and walls
    The tints of morning shine,
It needs not Love's muezzin calls
    To bid me seek their shrine.

From heart to heart, an eager tide,
    Pulses the mystic wine,
In such fair channel to abide
    And blend all mine and thine.

That out of Love's divine excess
    New life and hope may spring;
Out of the spirit's loving stress
    New songs, new souls to sing.

Out of his rare array of tints
  The artist, deft and true,
Upon a fresher fabric prints
  Thy loveliness anew.

So time and space, by Love impearled,
  Are swallowed up in bliss,
A Cleopatra draught, a world
  Dissolving in a kiss!

THE MUSIC CURE

AH, Doctor, your hand! So! And now, as I hold
This palm that I value so truly,
Here's a bill for your bill, though I warrant that gold
  Cannot pay all my debt to you duly.

Yes, I need you no longer; the pain I endured
  Has vanished, I hope, now, forever.
You will laugh when I tell you the way I was cured —
  By contracting a more ardent fever!

You have heard how the women are thronging the ways
  That lead up to fame and position;
And I know you will frown when I join in the praise
  Of fair woman in guise of physician.

As I stopped by a door one fine morning in May,
  A song through the doorway came trilling
And down to the core of my heart made its way,
  Like a tonic both healing and thrilling.

It seemed to say : "Live not for self, but for me,
  And your heart will beat easy hereafter."
So she cured me with song, and with smiles set me
    free,
  And such dear counter-irritant laughter !

Now, given that one has a palpitant heart,
  Is not a soft pressure pacific ?
And, if taken between meals, with delicate art,
  Are not kisses a fine soporific ?

You said once my heart had expanded too wide ;
  So I thought, as it was over-roomy,
I might as well take a dear lady inside —
  And 'tis glad now, where once it was gloomy.

I wish that I could but portray you my prize —
  All the grace of my dear little singer —
But I stop in despair at her beautiful eyes !
  No, I cannot describe her ! I'll bring her !

Now, Doctor, don't envy this rival of yours,
  With her pharmacopœia of beauty,
Since her voice and her eyes work such marvel-
    ous cures,
  To love my new doctor is duty.

LOVE

THERE are only four letters in " Love,"
    Yet how fully it speaks for the heart !
How liquid it drops from the tongue
  As it lets the lips kiss once and part !

For love is a lore of itself ;
  The sages, unschooled in its ways,
Though they know all the books on the shelf,
  Are but simpletons still all their days.

LOVE

Breath of flower, gleam of gem, song of bird,
  Blush of blossom of Dawn or of cheek —
Still it's love that's the one magic word
  That they all wait to hear or to speak.

The planets that never rebel,
  The seasons that, laughing, join hands;
The showers that the breezes compel,
  All listen to love's own commands.

When bird crosses bird in the air,
  When rose leans to rose in the vale,
When lad nods to lass on the stair,
  They are writing but love's magic tale.

When the universe first had its birth,
  Unto love as a pledge it was given.
There's nothing more lovely on earth —
  There's nothing more holy in heaven.

For love has held beautiful sway
  Since the sun dropped his first golden bars,
And love is as fresh as the day
  Because it is old as the stars.

AMONG THE DAISIES

DOWN among the daisies,
    All the summer day,
Katydids and beetles
  And grasshoppers play.
Did you never lie on the grass and list
  To the murmur and motion of the life below?
I should not wonder if they laughed and kissed —
  They might as well, for who would ever know
What they did among the daisies?

Down among the daisies,
　We together lie:
Only you and I, dear,
　And nobody nigh.
Lift up your eyelids, bonny little Miss!
　To guess my riddle you are slow.
Well, you know I am waiting for a kiss —
　We might as well, for who will ever know
What we do among the daisies?

AT LAKE GEORGE

UPON the Horicon's calm breast
　　All day we sailed and dreamed,
Idly, as o'er Black Mountain's crest
　　The gray clouds slowly streamed.

The circling hills stood firm and strong,
　　Like brothers banded there
In silent guard lest any wrong
　　The lake, their sister fair.

Up through the water to the eye
　　The shining pebbles showed;
Sweet was the air, and sweetly by
　　The hours, like ripples, flowed.

Then did I find a clearer deep
　　Reflected in your eye,
Where thoughts, like islands, half asleep,
　　Drowsed in serenity.

So seemed your life so like the lake,
　　As potent to allure!
May it as gently sleep and wake,
　　As fair, as deep, as pure.

AN EVOLUTION

IN a nebula of Thought,
   By my table I am sitting,
   Fairy visions round me flitting,
All refusing to be caught.

Now, a flash of charming eyes,
   Now, some witchery of dress,
   Or some hidden loveliness,
Comes and gleams and fades and dies.

And I wonder if this dream
   Of lovely forms and angel eyes
   Will not change and crystallize
To a joy that does not seem.

Softly swings the door ajar,
   Tender voice my soul is waking,
   And a kiss my dream is breaking,
Nebula has changed to star!

CROSSING ONTARIO

ON one of grand-dame's old blue bowls
   There sailed a maid and her Lothario,
'Twas you and I — so Time unrolls —
Crossing the blue bowl of Ontario.

These trails of smoke are but pipe-wreaths
   Blown out by some occult Canadian
Who o'er this bowl of coffee breathes
   In after-dinner bliss Arcadian.

Oh, yes, a quite extensive bowl!
   Perhaps he lifts it by some leverage,
But then it's not so large, dear soul,
   For you to sweeten all the beverage!

That French girl has such pretty lips —
 Were I the guardsman, I would want to —
Keep still? All right. The blue bowl tips!
 And we are landed in — Toronto.

A LOVING CUP
 (To C. U. P.)

A LOVING cup! Ah, could I fill
 The slender measure of my line
With that delicious, witching wine
Your autumn-tinted eyes distil,
 Then while my muse should gayly trip,
  My door I'd dup
 To radiant memories, and sip
  A loving cup!

Go, take your glass, and looking there,
Confess your face is wondrous fair!
Then wonder when I tell you true
'Tis fairer far to me than you.
 For now it fills my heart with joy,
  Now drinks it up!
 Why should you treat it like a toy —
  A loving cup?

A VISIT FROM THE MUSE

SHE dropped in by my study fire,
  And keeping still lest I offend her,
I watched the genius of my lyre —
 Her little feet were on the fender.

" I just came in to learn the news, —
 Now never mind about your pencil;

A VISIT FROM THE MUSE

When I grant regular 'interviews'
 I give them all cut out with stencil!"

She sighed and said she lonesome grew,
 Upon the hill where she was staying.
Parnassus held a varied crew, —
 She'd rather by herself be straying.

Loose sandaled, with her gold bronze hair
 Resting like sunshine on her shoulder,
She seemed so wise, demure, and fair,
 I gazed, admired, and then grew bolder.

"You make me proud, fair damozel,
 Me on so dark a night to visit.
Are you the maid who serves me well
 Or she who flouts me? Pray which is it?'

" I charm or plague you as I please.
 Why, sir, I thought you'd been a lover!"
I think she knew, the little tease,
 Phyllis was in the room above her.

"And now," said she, "did you work out
 The thought I sent you, Tuesday morning?"
I blushed and she began to pout.
 "Forgot it!" Ah, that look of scorning!

"They come so fast that in arrears
 I fain must get. I know 'tis wicked,
I can't find words to dress the dears
 And I can't show the cherubs naked."

She laughed right out. I saw her eyes,
 Gray, grave, and sweet, of that I'm certain,
With smiles, like children, bashful wise,
 Playing about each silken curtain.

We talked until she rose to leave,
　　I told her poetry sold slowly,
She said there was less cause to grieve,
　　It showed I loved it for her wholly.

How Aldrich penned his Eastern dreams,
　　How Volk his Winter idylls painted,
We touched on these and other themes
　　Until we got quite well acquainted.

Comparing things that pleased our tastes,
　　Great open fires and cloudy weather,
And forest walks and winter wastes,
　　We found our thoughts ran well together.

Before I knew it she had flown,
　　Ere I had kissed her! What a pity!
But I sat down right there alone,
　　And wrote in praise of her this ditty.

THE OFFER

TAKE thou my songs, O constant Friend of
　　　Friends!
They are the bubbles on my stream of years,—
　　They are the blossoms of my richest field.
Through them I rove where fair Walloomsac
　　　bends,
　　And see deep, dove-like eyes, all smiles and
　　　tears,
　　　Reflected in my heart as in a shield.

Photograph by R. H. Moulton.

"Watching the reaper in the harvest field."

— *In Midsummer.*

SONNETS

IN MIDSUMMER

Watching the reaper in the harvest field —
The mingled pathos of the falling grain,
And Summer's glory, now so soon to wane —
A new life-picture seems to me revealed : —
How gently Nature's leading is concealed !
 How deftly she deceives the eye and brain,
 While airs and scents, intoxicating, feign
A youth time in the Year so soon to yield !

As we implore no Season to delay,
 But follow eagerly the brave advance
  Of bird and bud, of kernel, fruit, and frost;
So, kindly, Fate beguiles our haunted way
 With dear Delusions, that before us dance
  And pipe the music of " The World Well Lost."

THE SONNET'S CHIME

Rare bells are they that form the Sonnet's chime,
 Swinging within the poet's open soul
 As in a belfry, from which grandly roll
Heart-melodies, entrancing or sublime.
In star-shine or in storm, time after time,
 Steal out invisible, in misty stole,
  The wingèd Thoughts and speed from pole to pole,
While sounds some golden, sweet, recurrent rhyme.

The Sonnet's chime is lofty, pure, and strong;
  Who rings it must climb patiently the stair,
  Winding about, past windows looking far.
Then one may ring so as to fright a Wrong,
  Or call a wandering soul to suppliant prayer,
  Or send Love's thrilling cry from star to star.

ASTERS AND GOLDENROD

THE year is like a king. In winter days
    He sheathes himself in ice, a glittering mail,
In which his enemies he may assail —
Guarding his throne in cold and bitter ways.
A king again, aside he quickly lays
    His helm and greaves when summer winds her frail
But potent spell about him in some dale
Where Nature acts her royal mimic plays.

Yet to his feet again, at touch of Frost,
    He leaps from dalliance, breathes the northern air,
Drinks deep the musk wine that the maids have trod,
And cries: "September, vassal, art thou lost?
    Ho! I am king; my royal robes I'll wear —
The purple aster and the goldenrod!"

MAY AND JUNE
(A Sonnet of Summer Time.)

MAY moves in her own perfume as she trips
    Across the fields, and with her footstep prints

The soft green page with flowers of bashful
    tints.
June in the color fount more deeply dips,
And paints his red on rose trees till it drips!
    May's pink upon a breast of whiteness glints,
    She teases us with promises and hints.
June puts the berry red between the lips.

At last they meet! One balmy soft midnight
    May yields to June the scepter of her power,
    Drops her sweet mystery and sweeter glows.
Ah, who can guess what secret vows they plight
    To speed the year when May yields up her
      dower
    Of blushing buds to June's unfolding rose!

ONE I KNOW

I KNOW a maiden in whose breast there lies
    A heart more pure than Himalaya's snows,
And sweeter than the spirit of a rose.
A child-like innocence dwells in her eyes,
Which lift unconsciously toward the skies
    When she is lost in thought; creation grows
    Daily more beautiful to her, and those
Who know her best say she is more than wise.

For all her life is peace and glad content;
    Believing good of all things, yet, like glass,
    Her spirit lets no hurt of evil pass,
Though free to all things that are innocent.
    So doth she live in unpretending grace,
    And daily blesses all who see her face.

CREASY'S "FIFTEEN BATTLES"

IN this thin book, that shows no crimson stain,
   We trace the course of empire flowing through
The ancient world until it meets the new.
And Saratoga mirrors back the plain
Of Marathon, while Blenheim's bloody rain
   Gives warning dire of weltering Waterloo.
   So, too, rise up, portentous to the view,
Hastings, Pultowa, Valmy's dreadful train!

How like a line of rugged beetling crags,
   That thrust a river to the left or right —
     And sometimes turn it back upon its course —
Loom up these battles! Likewise never flags
   The human heart-beat, like the river's might,
     Winning its Freedom, spite of any Force.

BY THE BURNED DWELLING

THE trees, like mourners, linger round the place
Where once the homelike country dwelling stood.
   Once did they wave their boughs in merry mood,
When children's voices echoed round the space,
But now their branches softly interlace
   In silent sympathy, as if they would
   Find solace, grateful to their hearts of wood,
For the lost comfort of a human face.

So sigh we o'er the idylls of the past,
   So mourn we, pensive, 'mid the falling leaves.
     So pine we, vainly, for the friends most dear.
Yet still a whisper says: Be not downcast.
   And to the heart that all too sorely grieves
     A voice shall say: Seek not your loved ones here.

WILHELMJ

O BRIGHT-SOULED brother from the Fatherland!
On thy broad brow we cannot fail to see
How royally Cecilia dowered thee
With scepter of a more than king's command!
We are but subjects as we see thee stand,
   Potent with music as a summer tree,
   While low, Æolian " Airs from Hungary "
Make our hearts flame from embers they have fanned!

And now we part; across the bank of flowers
   We look farewell with music's mutual glance;
Soon shall the chorus of the care-worn Hours
   Replace the strains that lately did entrance;
Yet ne'er shall die the echoes of thy bow,
   Nor from our hearts cans't thou, Wilhelmj, go!

CONSCIENCE

HOW fair she lies in her soft-lidded sleep!
   So step but lightly, let her take her ease,
Who sleep do well! Can we her better please?
And meanwhile are there any laws to keep?
If she be mistress, 'twill be time to weep
   When she doth chide us; we may then appease
   By saying sin is sin but when one sees,
And sheep will roam when shepherds slumber deep!

Then doth the sleeper open angel eyes,
   With strange, deep meaning, showing that she heard
   Our foolish babble, knew our every deed!

In that sad look what keen arraignment lies,
  What Sinai thunders in her whispered word, —
  The patient Friend we wrong when most we need!

OFTEN I LEAVE THEE

OFTEN I leave thee, Love, and wend my way
  Among the many strangers on the street,
  And as I scan each fair one that I meet,
Their gliding forms, their various features' play,
And charms elusive, to myself I say:
  "This lady's smile doth flash out very sweet,"
  Or, "There are angel's eyes," or, "How complete
A charm doth yonder Dian form convey!"

But all these fickle fancies from me flee
  When, hasting homeward with the setting sun,
Thy perfect self reminds me that in thee
  I hold all beauties since the race begun;
And how much dearer these delights to me
  To feel that they are all contained in one!

MARY ANDERSON

MILLIONS of men have said: "Her face is fair,"
  And so say travelers, sailing down a stream,
  Of some grand palace, lovely as a dream,
Set on the shore, outlined against the air.

But little do such far-off gazers share
   The mansion's beauty, catching not a gleam
   Of that interior charm that makes it seem,
To those who know it, rich beyond compare.

Yes, thou art fair, but they have higher praise
   Who thy rich-treasured mind have looked upon
And seen thee actress of thy own sweet will!
Yet now art thou bereft us many days,
   And even the Public, thy Pygmalion,
   Doth mourn its Galatea, lost and still!

TO VENUS

IF, haply, when our sun has reached its west,
   And Night comes, stealthy, stealing o'er our souls,
It should be our last destiny to rest
   Where the blue arc its spangled field unrolls;
If such should chance to be my fortune bright,
   I would not seek the side of yon North Star
To watch the revels of the orbs of light
   And catch their music coming from afar.

No, I would hie to thee, sweet planet-bride,
   And in thy silver smile be amply blest,
There to behold thee charm the eventide
   Till lovers sped to put their love to test;
Nor care how lordly Jupiter might ride,
   Or swift Orion push his endless quest.

POEMS OF HOME-LIFE, ETC.

AN HOUR OF SONG

AN Hour of Song! Perchance it shall be fleeter
   For knowing it shall not detain us long.
So fleet the moments! Yet they shall be fleeter
   If winged with music in an Hour of Song.

A Song of Childhood! Raise the artless numbers
   That rhyme with brooks and flowers and busy birds;
With merry romps, with angel-guarded slumbers,
   With joy that laughs at inexpressive words.

A Song of Youth and Love's divine delusion —
   The strong, pure faith in one fair kindred soul —
The touch that turns the world's poor, sad confusion
   To true delight, harmonious and whole!

A Song of Strife, of teeth set hard together,
   Of hearts that press against the spear of fate;
Of helms that swerve not in the blackest weather;
   Of lips that smile their high contempt of hate!

Ah, sing the riches we may keep forever —
   The kiss, the smile, the song, the sky above —
The friendships held so high that friends can never
   By any act deprive them of our love!

Sing then, who can! Soon to our duller senses
   A Silence on the Song and Singer falls;
Yet who shall say with what fine recompenses
   The sounds may haunt the Soul's eternal halls?

"A Song of Youth and Love's divine delusion —
The strong pure faith in one fair kindred soul."
— *An Hour of Song.*

An Hour of Song! Your hands, dear ones, extending,
   Join in the chorus, fair and full and strong;
Brave voices in the last dear moment blending —
   So brief and sweet is life — An Hour of Song!

OLD-FASHIONED FLOWERS

OLD-FASHIONED flowers! They linger round the dwelling
   Like gentle memories of spirits blest;
With kindly faces, lovely odors, telling
   Of hands that tended them, now gone to rest.

How fair they look against the old gray shingles!
   No palace could compare with yonder cot,
Where the dark green with purple lilac mingles
   In harmony that cannot be forgot.

Old-fashioned flowers! They line our garden closes
   With yearly charms, like ever-constant friends;
The pansies smile up at the stately roses,
   The aster with the phlox its beauty blends.

Ah, maidens! Do not scorn grandmother's beauties!
   No prouder title could ye win for dowers,
Than — making life more sweet by lowly duties —
   To grow, each day, more like old-fashioned flowers.

Old-fashioned flowers, old-fashioned friends and faces,
   Old-fashioned love, the one true dearest heart!
The breath of roses brings me back your graces
   With sweet assurance they shall ne'er depart.

OUR ROUND TABLE

How often, in the days now fled,
We've seen our homely table spread,
And gathered to the simple meal
With pleasure we would not conceal!
Though not for us the costly wines,
The red heart-tribute of the vines,
Yet richer draught, from purer skies,
We drink from loved, familiar eyes.
What though our fare is plain, indeed,
It yet is plenty to our need;
We count each presence at the feast
More precious far than all the East,
With spice, and sweets, and golden ore,
Might bring us from her richest shore.
Our dishes old, of quaint design,
Will never cause us to repine;
The chippings in the ancient stone
Will help each one to tell his own.
The homespun linen is as white
As snowfields on a winter night;
Our candle lights as honest faces
As ever met in kingly places;
For jewels, youthful eyes and old
Flash out a wealth that ne'er was told;
For which we hold in high disdain
The gems of Good Alraschid's reign.
Stranger, 'twould do you good to see
Our hearty, homebred company;
When, gathering from the haunts of strife,
We enter in our sweet home-life.
The fervent grace, but briefly said,
Unloads each heart, while bows each head;
And then all round the happy place
Love's language flies from face to face,
With smile and laughter, pun and jest,
And kindly act and sweet request.

Mixed with adventures of the day,
The grave discussion and the gay;
Thus ready thought, fleet-winged with sound,
Our Mercury, speeds the cup around.
A health then, knights and ladies all,
Who gather in our festal hall!
Here's Enid and here's Imogen,
Both fair and gracious to our ken;
Here's to our Arthur and Geraint,
To patron and to mother saint!
We drink to all who couch their spears
In honor of these later years
When eyes too often lose the fire
Enkindled by some knightly sire.
Believe me, 'tis not yet grown cold,
The blood that fired the days of old!
For though we ply our peaceful arts,
We wear our crests upon our hearts,
And he who throws deriding glance
Meets shining shield and level lance!

LINES
(With a Book by J. M. Barrie.)

AS some brave, warm-hearted rill,
   Though ice-prisoned, works its will;
Melting, melting, through the hours,
Till its margins burst in flowers;
So a vein of Scottish blood
Surely brings its banks to bud
And to bloom with blossoms fair —
Kindness, humor debonair.
Since, then, underneath the mask
Of our English names there bask
Streams that savor more of sun,
Strains from ancient clansmen run,

Fit it is I ask you tarry
Here at "Tillyloss" with Barrie —
Painter rare of Scotland's wiles,
Scotland's tears and Scotland's smiles!

BABY'S PARADISE

IT'S always blue in the baby's sky;
    No matter how clouds are hurled,
The clear blue lens of the baby's eye
    Makes heaven of all the world!

She hardly knew when she came to earth;
    The buds and the voices kind
And the dappled light that met her birth
    Seemed just what she left behind.

If she should vanish on snowy wing
    On a June day fair and rich,
Hear first the robins, then angels, sing,
    She'd wonder: "Now which is which?"

And what if angels, who came to greet
    This waif from the world so new,
Should hear her murmur, so baby-sweet:
    "My mamma's as pretty as you"?

TO A SPARROW

POOR, lonely, little fluffy thing!
    A gray mite in the cold and sleet,
With glossy head and folded wing,
    Soft cuddling down upon your feet!

You know not if the morrow's sun
    May find you frozen on that bough;
And don't you wonder, pretty one.
    Where your next meal is waiting now?

Gaily you chirp and dodge the storm,
   And turn your head and prune your wing.
Strange that from such a tiny form
   So large a lesson there should spring!

I, who, well sheltered, often pine;
   I, who, sometimes, have food to spare,
Am fain to join my fate with thine
   If I might in thy spirit share.

Brave little bird! I thank you now
   For the new courage I have found,
As I remember such as thou
   Fall not unnoticed to the ground.

TRUST

PLAYING and shouting all the morning
      hours,
Crying, perhaps, with pain or childish grief,
Wayward as humming-birds among the flowers,
   Busy as builders of the coral reef;

So prattles on my rosy little lad.
   Can I forgive him that he drives away
Thought from the subject, pencil from the pad?
   Ah, little man, soon comes the sleep, I say.

Sudden I note that all around is still,
   Unvexed my ear by laughter wild and sweet,
Unhindered now my pen may have its will —
   There lies my darling, close about my feet.

Thus, while forgetting what I meant to write,
   Mayhap I learn a lesson far more deep:
Father of all! When comes for us the night,
   May we so trustfully lie down to sleep!

A DIAMOND

        Musing
        I lie;
       My eye
    Piercing the gloom
    To yonder room
 Where round the evening lamp
  Lies our domestic camp.
Bivouacked about, each with some task,
 In the warm, golden light they bask.
The sisters bend above their study books
The brother reads, and mother, with sweet looks
Her glasses cannot hide, is busy with her knitting;
Father, with meerschaum pipe and paper, near her
        sitting.
  I would that I might keep forevermore
   The picture as I see it through the door:
    For, by its aid, in some dark hour,
    I may discern, by the same power,
      In one fair horoscope
      Love, memory, and hope
       Around some light,
       And make life bright
         When I
         Shall lie
         Musing.

STELLA

Home from the observatory,
   Now I take her on my knee,
And I tell her all the glory
   That the lenses showed to me.
Pleased, she listens to my story,
   Earnest look then turneth she

Where the stars are softly blinking
    In the blue of summer skies.
Ah! She sees beyond my thinking,
    Even into Paradise!
Very humbly I am drinking
    What o'erfloweth from her eyes.

TO CLARISE

DAME NATURE, one delightful day,
    Cried: "Bring to me my choicest clay;
I'll make a maid to suit myself,
In spite of Fate, the ugly elf."
So grew the maid, and all the while
Dame Nature worked she wore a smile.
"Not very large, nor very tall,
The rarest things are often small.
Light, supple, strong, my maid shall be —
Swift as a Dian on the lea.
I'll give her just a winsome face,
Wearing a touch of old-time grace;
A forehead wide and fair to view,
Thin nostrils, telling blood that's blue;
Firm, gentle mouth, eyes keen and kind,
Lamps fit to light a lovely mind."
Then Nature said: "If it's no sin,
I will show I can make a chin."
She turned it full and strong and round,
And, lo! the face was fitly bound;
Then crowned the whole with dark brown hair,
And viewed her maiden, standing there.

"Now you must be a new example
Among my models, fair and ample;
You shall delight in country lanes,
Where move the fragrant, loaded wains:

Yet all the more shall you be fit
To charm the town with grace and wit,
To cheer the weak, to tame the strong,
Or melt them all with smile and song.
But ever shall your heart be true
To the green meadows tipped with dew.
You shall the highest prize in books
The mirrored truth of Nature's looks,
And children in your face shall view
Proof of a comrade blithe and true.
And more, I know my girl shall be
A thrifty type of housewifery,
A master hand in every part,
Lifting up drudgery to art."
So Nature spoke, and passed from view;
The maiden wondered where she flew.
But evermore between the twain
The bond of love did wax amain;
Oft did the maiden list to hear
Some whispered hint of Nature near;
While Nature touched to lovelier grace
The charm of mind and form and face.

TWO SISTERS

I REMEMBER a home by the hillside,
    And a little room, curtained, within;
I see through the laces two sisters,
    And one holds her dear violin.

She's a sister one could not but covet,
    With dark eyes that silently speak;
Her violin, how she does love it!
    I envy it there by her cheek.

Of the other, the silver soprano,
   I scarce could tell all the sweet truth;
But she looks there, before the piano,
   Like a dream of the spirit of youth.

The soft-blending music comes stealing,
   And I wonder if those sisters guess
How they're filling my heart up with feeling,
   Which I never, with words, can express.

And now into silence 'tis dying —
   Aye, it died many long days ago;
Yet the echoes will often come flying
   When the soft winds of memory blow.

They tell of a music diviner
   Which those who reach heaven shall find,
Which I fully believe will be finer,
   Yet I cannot imagine its kind.

So I hope for forgiveness when, sometimes,
   I think how that music will seem,
If a voice, violin, and piano
   Shall mingle within my dream.

A SILVER WEDDING
(To W. P. E.)

YEARS with the silver feet,
   Years with the pinions fleet,
What do you bring to-night?
Frost in the thick brown hair,
Thought in the furrows of care,
   Sown in the day and night.

Years with the sandals gray,
What have ye taken away?

All the fortune unkind,
All the trial and pain,
Never to come again.
  Leaving the love behind.

Years, you make all amends,
Bringing us troops of friends,
  With many a silvery word.
Yet deep in the well-tried heart
Lieth the gold apart —
  Wealth to others unheard.

A GOLDEN WEDDING
(To S. N.)

No chartered right is mine to speak
  The words of love when friends are meeting,
Yet truth, which brightens gifts most meek,
  May gild my greeting.

For if to not another cause
  My lines for merit were beholden,
Your names would make, spite of all flaws,
  A picture golden.

It seems that while the Golden State
  Since " Forty-nine " has drawn men thither,
To-night, for you, the Golden Gate
  Has journeyed hither.

Thus fifty years, like fifty streams,
  Have yielded ore in changeful weather,
Since when you staked, 'mid happy dreams,
  Your claim together.

And now to overflow your till, —
  No need to rise and pass the platter! —
The nuggets of our warmest will
  We gladly scatter.

Wise Argonauts! Like you we might
  Be wealthy, if we could divine it —
How our own lives with gold are bright
  If we would mine it.

And through those fifty years unrolled —
  Can you not see it brightly glinting,
The wondrous, precious, priceless gold
  Of love's own minting?

Well may you join the song and laugh,
  And hope with us, with hearts the lightest,
The century's coming other half
  May be the brightest.

THANKSGIVING DAY

NOT once a year, but every day,
  With hearts by gratitude grown tender,
Would we thus pause upon our way
  And praise and thanks unto Thee render.

Yet in this harvest of the year,
  We come, with hearts o'er full, confessing
How all our land is filled with cheer
  And all our coasts bask in Thy blessing.

Then let us all survey our past,
  And note Thy guidance to our living,
Till each confesses he, at last,
  Has greatest cause for true thanksgiving.

THE FRESH AIR CHILDREN

WHO are these pilgrims, eager-eyed,
    One sees on every hand,
Like travelers who have wandered wide
    Now in their chosen land?

Their pleading looks have power to pry
    The rich man's safe apart;
The frosts, before their laughter, fly
    Off from the farmer's heart.

True little missionaries they,
    Who journey up and down,
And bind in closer sympathy
    The country and the town.

For children scatter blessings
    Ever — since they were blessed —
And their unconscious sermons
    Excel the preacher's best.

God sets a little child above
    The sage of deepest sense;
Not what we know, but what we love,
    Is Heavenly Evidence.

TICK–TOCK!

ALL day, tick-tock, the great clock on the wall!
All day, tick-tock, the big clocks and the small!
O clock-man, clock-man, make our clocks tick right!
So that they keep time with thine all the day and night.

TICK-TOCK!

All day, beat, beat, — the great Heart over all!
All day, beat, beat, — the big hearts and the small.
O Wise One, Wise One, make our hearts beat right,
So that they keep time with thine all the day and night.

FARM POEMS, DIALECT, ETC.

PLOWING

>What time the cock, the plowman's horn,
>Wakens the lily-wristed morn.—*Herrick*.

GOOD mornin', sir! A clearin' sky—
What? Want to talk with me, sir?
You tracked across that piece o' rye,
  But we won't disagree, sir.

I'm sure you're welcome on this sod.
  The piece was heavy-seeded;
The finest catch there, where you trod,
  Since the old farm was deeded.

Whoa, boy! It's gettin' warm ag'in—
  That colt is just a-learnin'—
Come, boy! Come, Fan, come in! Come in!
  They're rather slow a-turnin'.

The air, I guess, don't smell so sweet
  Where you live, in the city,
No grass or shade-trees on the street?
  Now, that must be a pity.

I calculate a farmer lacks
  Some things you make a show of;
But there may be some curious facts
  That city folks don't know of.

You see the nest on that pine bough?
  Do you know what there's hid in't?
D'ye know what bird 'tis singin' now?
  No? Well, I thought you didn't.

PLOWING

You mus'n't think a pleasin' thing
   Is lost on country people;
The birds that in that maple sing
   Beat chimes in any steeple.

And as for good, fresh thinkin' stuff,
   Paved streets can't be so givin';
While this one field has got enough
   To last you while you're livin'.

Kin Boston beat that row of stumps
   The little lot is fenced with?
Who-o-o-a! Woodchuck holes are wuss'n mumps!
   The beasts might be dispensed with.

You'd like to hold the plow awhile?
   All right, sir. I am willin'.
Whoa, there, I say! Don't go a mile!
   You'd ought to kept its bill in.

What threw the plow out? Oh, a stone.
   They're rather apt to turn her.
I guess I'll go it best alone —
   You do well for a learner.

Why, I have seen men lean and try
   To push the plow before 'em!
'Twould make a horse laugh till he'd cry;
   But one fool makes a quorum.

I s'pose they think that Kingdom Come
   Depends on them for motion;
But of the Power that's pullin' some
   They haven't the slightest notion.

It's like good times to plow sod loam,—
   To hear the coulter rippin',
And the soft earth, like fallin' foam,
   Into the furrer drippin'.

But when you strike a stretch o' stone
   It's sickness and low prices!
The plow not only shakes each bone
   But kinder wakes yer vices.

A plow's a contrary concern,
   A young calf can't outdo it;
To guide the point the handles turn
   The opposite way to it.

Cut furrer wide, lean handles right —
   You know how 'tis, I dare say —
Lift up, and it dives out of sight,
   And t'other way, vice versey.

Not married? Well, you'll hardly swim
   Before you go in swimmin';
But p'raps you'll find that in this whim
   A plow is like some wimmin!

Nags like the furrer — softer ground —
   Their crowdin's apt to balk us;
They're like two politicians bound
   To carry the same caucus.

The colt lags, don't he? 'Pon my soul,
   I guess the mare's the stronger!
I'll move that clevis up a hole
   And make his end the longer.

Young hoss, if you don't stop that prank
   I'm 'fraid you'll get a floggin'.
This knoll grows quack-grass mighty rank —
   The meanest stuff for cloggin'!

I'm blamed if quack-grass ain't like sin,
   It grows where land's the poorest;
Ag'in a hoe it's sure to win —
   Guess buryin's the surest.

PLOWING

I tried a new plow at the fair;
    'Twas neat, but I refused it.
This "Rough and Ready" stands the tear,
    And our folks allus used it.

Old plows and old beliefs are strong,
    And good yet if kept shinin'!
Things that have stood the strain so long
    Kin stand some underminin'.

I like to watch before the plow
    The grass a-tumblin' over;
The big and little have to bow,
    The June-grass and the clover.

A plow reminds me, then, of Time.
    Does't other folks, I wonder?
There goes a violet in its prime —
    I hate to turn them under.

But when above the buried weeds
    The yellow wheat is wavin',
'Twill teach that buried years and deeds
    Still live, if worth the savin'.

A lifetime dwindles like these lands
    In which the lot's divided;
When the dead-furrer's reached one stands
    And wonders where it's slided.

Tell how I run a furrer straight,
    And keep my sights when sowin'?
Yer competition would be late,
    So I don't mind yer knowin'.

I set that pole this side the lot,
    Then start from over yonder,
And range that pole with some fur spot
    And never let it wander.

I've sometimes thought if we would range
    Our daily walk with Natur',
Our lives with things that never change,
    We'd draw our furrer straighter.

I'm apt at preachin'? So I've heard.
    Yes, I 'tend church on Sunday.
Why, if I didn't hear the Word
    I couldn't work on Monday.

Ah, ha! That whistle blows for noon,
    And dinner-time, I'm thinkin';
Well, I don't think it blows too soon,—
    I feel like eatin' an' drinkin'.

Ned's callin' me, my little son,—
    Jest five years ter his story;—
He makes us seven, countin' one
    That's now a child o' glory.

How proud that team steps now that they
    Are p'intin' for the stable!
A pretty tune their trappin's play,
    Judgin' as I am able.

Come in the house and see my Nell —
    I think she ain't bad lookin'—
And she's just as reliable
    At counselin' as cookin'!

A SONG OF THE DRUDGE

A SONG in my heart keeps on ringing to-day,
    Though I fear me the old cry of "fudge"!
Yet a bard has one merit — he will have his say —
    And my song is A Song of the Drudge.

A SONG OF THE DRUDGE

Yes, even the toilers in kitchen and hall —
  The many who strike not nor shirk, —
I fancy a halo encircles them all —
  The crown of the Honor of Work!

For there must be some who will gird up the skirt,
  And take up the tasks that are mean,
And valiantly conquer the kingdom of dirt
  That the rest of mankind may be clean.

For the scavenger's hoe, and his pail, and his broom,
  Are the mystical scepters of health;
And nothing beside them can long keep the bloom
  On the cheeks of the children of wealth.

Since Prometheus got up that first early fire —
  The precursor of many a smudge —
How many have swallowed their ease or their ire
  To do that first task of the drudge!

And how many by that fire have roasted themselves,
  With their beefsteaks have sizzled and broiled,
To see that provision for us — lucky elves —
  Was properly stewed, baked, or boiled!

Ah, the drudge! It is he who lifts up from the earth
  Many lives into fortunate ways:
And it may be his work is sometimes of more worth
  Than the poet's who sings in his praise.

There's our brother, the "Hayseed," who lives on
    the farm,
  With his plow and his pitchfork and flail,
Who must toil on, or cities would soon come to
    harm,
  Should the "Hayseed" or hay ever fail!

Dear me! It is nice to be called Ph. D.,
  Or letters of any such ilk,
Yet if every one boasted a college degree,
  There would still be the cattle to milk.

O Drudges! Look up to the heavenly blue,
  For your honors we may not rehearse
When post-graduate titles are showered upon
    you
  At commencement of God's universe.

So, ladies, one moment from whist and from
    wine,
  And you — minister, doctor, or judge, —
Join all in a toast to this hero of mine: —
  Long life to our brother — the Drudge!

"THE LAST DAY OF SCHOOL"

TO-DAY I saw upon the street
    A crowd of children, poor, yet neat,
Flocking to school with willing feet,
  In the summer morning cool.
This day they all will look their best,
And do their tasks with willing zest,
For now has come vacation's rest,
  'Tis the "Last day of school."

"THE LAST DAY OF SCHOOL"

It sets me thinking of the days
When I, too, loitered through learning's ways;
Less fond of books than schoolboy plays,
    Always eager for fun!
The hill of knowledge was steep to me;
I much preferred to climb a *tree*,
Or, winters, skate the ice so free,
    And through the deep snow run!

'Twas full as hard in summer time
To watch that ledge of rocky lime
Where berries were just in their "prime,"
    And *birds* were free to pick them!
To "go in swimming," how we pined!
How late the sun at the western blind!
And those dull books, we had a mind,
    Well, just to kick them!

"Old sow and pigs" was quite a game —
Unless some whack should make you lame —
And "two-old-cat" is sure of fame
    As any bard of Greece.
Our studies? Oh, let's pass them by!
Farewell old "Bullions," too, but I
Remember when I "cut a pie"
    At playing "Fox and Geese."

Ink-bottles whizzing on their course
Would illustrate mysterious force —
We might be flogged till we were hoarse —
    We never could explain.
Again, ere we could dine or sup,
Some infant "Little Buttercup"
Would mix our frugal luncheons up —
    To our chagrin and pain.

A tribute to the dear old girls
Who lost our knives and stole our curls,
And set our cardiac tide in whirls
   With some soft-whispered word!
Walking and singing down the aisles,
With arms entwined and rosy smiles,
Ah, happy queens! Ah, witching wiles!
   (The lines are getting blurred.)

You notice I am country bred,
Of course our school was painted red;
Pine trees their needles near it shed —
   For bare feet quite a boon.
High hills we coasted in December,
Just far enough off, I remember,
To tempt each mischief-minded member
   To run away at noon!

I've ne'er seen wood that felt so hard
As those pine benches cut and scarred,
With many a rude initial marred —
   The dunces had a stool.
With a big red stove to scorch my face,
And a sharp-edged shelf my back to brace,
Do you wonder I prayed with fervent grace
   For the " Last Day of School "?

Ah, well! The longest school terms cease;
At last it came — our glad release:
But first each lad must " speak his piece,"
   In halting, sing-song rhymes.
The "trustee" came to watch the boys.
Sundry neighbors to hear the noise.
And criticise our bashful poise.
   Ah, those were good old times!

NO PARADISE FOR ANIMALS

"NO heaven for brutes," you fancy that is clear;
    Then let us make a heaven for them here!
If immortality is thus denied
To any beast beyond the Stygian tide,
Then all the more incumbent doth it seem
To make their earthly life a happy dream.
To be a horse is not to even know
One is "a horse," but just to daily grow
From frisky colthood to the proud estate
Of the tall steed that bears his master's weight.
To be a horse may either be to bear
Curses and loads and blows with meekest air;
Or it may be to feel a happy sense
Of serving gladly man's intelligence,
Eager, all times, to serve his owner's end,
And feel that godlike man is even his friend.
No, the poor animal may never trace
His line, as we our prehistoric race,
But, ah, how well he weighs our every tone,
Checked by a whisper, startled by a moan.
None like our patient, plodding servant knows
So well the difference 'twixt caress and blows.
The meaning of a cold or cozy stall
Is misery or comfort, that is all.
Not every mouth is suited with its bit.
Not all the food that's thrown to beasts is fit.
If Pegasus were galled or starved in ration
He'd bear no bards to mounts of inspiration.
Kick Rover out of doors, neglect to bone him,
He'll fawn on strangers, growl at those who own
    him.

No brutes in heaven? Well, then, so let it be,
The human animal must need agree,
Though wondering at the love that takes his soul,
All marred with sin, to the eternal goal,

And yet denies the patient slave in reins
Chance to disport on those Elysian plains.
Mayhap the rest is best for weary horses,
Mayhap among those far celestial forces
And high delights we shall not miss a pet,
Nor ever eye for a lost steed be wet.
But if it be the seers may be mistaken,
If noble quadrupeds in heaven may waken;
If, too, like Balaam's beast, their speech regained,
They tell when we have petted them or pained,
We'll not regret the days we gave their fill
Of goodly oats, or helped them up a hill!

Resting with higher Power if shall survive
The beasts He made in beauteous forms alive,
I yet declare that if I do not change,
I still should seek them on that higher range
Of Life Revived; should feel my eyes o'erfill
At whinnied greeting from some heavenly hill;
Or some lost collie, faithful to the end,
Wagging a welcome to his earthly friend.

"JENNIE B"

WELL I love to sing thy beauty,
   Jennie B,
And 'tis but a pleasant duty,
   Jennie B,
To tell how no wind nor weather
Ever strained the subtle tether
That has bound us two together —
   Jennie B.

"JENNIE B"

Ah, what pleasant miles we've traveled,
      Jennie B!
And what winding roads unraveled,
      Jennie B;
When the merry sun was beaming,
Or the gentle moon was dreaming,
Or the jagged lightning gleaming —
      Jennie B!

How one little word can move thee,
      Jennie B,
With a speed that doth behoove thee,
      Jennie B!
When thy rivals show their faces
As a challenge to thy paces,
Then how passing are thy graces —
      Jennie B.

For thy blood is of the bluest,
      Jennie B,
And thy step is of the truest,
      Jennie B.
To my ears there comes no greeting
Gladder than the rhythmic beating
Of thy nimble footsteps fleeting —
      Jennie B.

Though thy ears are ever ready,
      Jennie B,
Yet thy tongue is ever steady,
      Jennie B.

Whatsoever cruel mutter
My tongue wag in, that may cut her,
Not an unkind word doth utter
        Jennie B.

And her breath is like the clover —
        Jennie B, —
When her neck is arching over —
        Jennie B.
As her hair falls on my shoulder,
With my arms I there enfold her,
And I hug her as I hold her —
        Jennie B !

Then thy soft, thin nostrils playing —
        Jennie B.
And thy brown eyes volumes saying —
        Jennie B ;
And thy dainty ankle peeping,
Would compel a monk to keeping
Compliments upon you heaping —
        Jennie B !

But blue eyes are jealous looking,
        Jennie B,
And my language are not brooking,
        Jennie B ;
Don't you think that she is silly
Thus to judge of us so illy,
When you're only my bay filly,
        Jennie B ?

DRIVING THE COLT

'TWAS a still midsummer day;
    Slowly came the great clouds gray
O'er the mountain chain,
And the wisest could not say
    Whether it would rain.

"Harry Percy," aged four,
Stood before the farmhouse door,
    Quite a handsome pony;
Sober, as if pondering o'er
    A roadway, steep and stony.

Then appeared a picture fair,
A little girl with raven hair,
    So sweet you ne'er could chide her;
And she stepped in the wagon there, —
    A little boy beside her.

Off they drove with spirits gay,
In the dreamy summer day,
    Round the valley-side;
Not so very far away,
    Just a little ride.

Apples red the road o'erhung,
In the grass the locust sung
    As they rode along;
All the hazy valley rung
    With the Summer song.

So they wound among the hills,
Rumbled o'er the bridgèd rills,
    By fields of oats and flax;
Through the woods, past ruined mills,
    And brawling cataracts.

Patiently the pony stands,
While he heaps the maiden's hands
   With berries black and sweet,
While laborers in the bottom-lands
   Go, whistling, through the wheat.

Round them waved the tasseled corn,—
Other fields were ready shorn
   Of their bearded grain;
Which in the barns was being borne
   As back they rode again.

Only a little ride, and yet
The "little boy" will ne'er forget,
   But rather think with pride,
Of her who trusted in his pet
   And went with him to ride.

And as the shadowy seasons glide,
The "little girl," by her fireside,
   May oft recall with joy,
The little horse, the little ride,
   And the little boy.

TOLD IN THE BASIN
(A Canal Idyl).

NOONTIME in Atlantic Basin—
   Sailor lads in greasy dress
Slid from spars of stately traders
   Down the forward hatch to mess.

Rattling chain and creaking tackle
   Smote no longer on the ear,
Dappled sunshine ran in ripples
   On the string-piece of the pier.

Even the grim grain elevators
   Seemed to stop their chronic din
Just to watch two people talking
   On the grain-boat, *Nellie Gwynne.*

  . . . .

" Doctor, howdy!   Glad to see you!
   Ah, the girl!   She's doin' well.
She'll be up on deck direckl'y;
   Have a smoke and stay a spell.

" Doctor, I'd give half a dollar
   If I jest could speak my thought;
But I can't string words together
   So's to thank ye as I ought.

" Why, if you knew all the story,
   How it happened, years ago,
Guess you wouldn't blame me swearin'
   That I couldn't let her go.

" Doctor, I could tell you some things
   That I never told a pal:
But I'll tell you since you didn't
   Let the fever take the gal.

" T'was in sixty-six I picked up
   All the loose change I could float.
And to keep it above water
   Bought an interest in this boat.

" Just the year before I'd married —
   Wife was never very strong —
So she stayed, sometimes, with her folks
   While I boated.   P'raps 'twas wrong.

" Right here, Doc., you mustn't gamble
   Anything was wrong with *her!*
Heaven bless her!   What's the matter
   With my eyes?   Sometimes they blur.

"So she stayed this time I'm tellin' —
　House was just b'low the locks —
While I took my turn at Buffalo
　By the elevator docks.

"Jim Deyoe was just beside me —
　You know how we tie together —
Jim I'd always counted on —
　Friend in any kind o' weather.

"Well, I'd just been to the office;
　Got a letter, too, from home;
Wife wrote she was feelin' lonesome —
　Kinder sick — she wish't I'd come.

"When I got down to the feeder,
　Gad! I trembled on my feet;
My boat lay behind a dozen —
　Jim's was takin' in the wheat!

"Why, 'twas days before I loaded,
　And it seemed my head would swim;
I've give up all other cussin'
　Just to damn that traitor — Jim.

"'Course he could have kept me by him —
　Loaded both boats, end and end —
But he took a mean advantage,
　Cut me loose as was his friend.

"No, I never asked the reason —
　That's the last I heard o' Jim —
There's a drink, though, that I owe him —
　Cup o' sorrer — to the brim!

"Well, I started back a' hopin',
　After all, things wasn't bad;
One hour thinkin' o' my woman —
　Then o' Jim and almost mad.

"Couldn't find a man with gumption,
　　Somehow, fit to run the boat;
And as captain I was holdin'
　　Fer the cargo when afloat.

"Ever much to star-gaze, Doctor?
　　I'd mind deck there in the night,
Hold the tiller and just watch 'em
　　Till they faded out o' sight.

"And I guess they made me patient,
　　Or I'd never stood it all;
Doc., when one is in a hurry,
　　Hang a mule and the canawl!

"Well, I missed her light a-burnin'
　　When we stopped above the locks,
I made one run fer that cottage —
　　In I goes and never knocks.

"Oh, you're used to jest such stories,
　　But I'll finish — once begun —
Most men never lose but one wife —
　　And I'll never lose but one.

"There were two a-waitin' fer me —
　　One was dead and one asleep;
She had left her little pictur',
　　In that girl fer me to keep.

"I have told ye all the story —
　　Jim's name, yes — t'was Jim Deyoe.
Yours, too? That's so — I forgot it —
　　Curus, ain't it now — by Joe!

"What? You knew him? He your father?
　　He the man? Go slow! you say
He fell off — drowned in the Hudson
　　When the towboat broke away?

"Say, I couldn't stand no triflin'!
　　But I've always stood the truth.
Jim! Jim Deyoe! Then it's gospel
　　He's the man that saved my Ruth.

"Why, when that big hawser parted,
　　All the boats began to spread,
Ruth fell in — then some one caught her —
　　But the boats closed o'er his head.

"Well, well, well! Now what's forgiveness?
　　I would throw Jim now a line,
But his dock's paid in a basin
　　When his craft's ahead o' mine.

"Doctor! There's your bill — you take it.
　　Make it foot a little more —
Savin' Ruth twice in succession —
　　But it can't be paid in ore.

"Eh? You want the girl? Well, really,
　　Now ye tech me! Well, well, well!
Guess the boat without the bird in
　　Would be like an empty shell.

"Ruth, sir? Why, she's like her mother —
　　Jest that trim-like, in her wrap —
When we go to th' floatin' chapel,
　　Or to hear old Halsey Knapp,

"You would see the people lookin'—
　　And I sized up what it meant —
That canal-boats could hold beauties
　　If they didn't pay high rent.

"Guess the gang-plank could tell stories
　　Of consid'able many feet
Come to visit Ruthie's cabin
　　Cos 'twas brightest in the fleet.

"But you're tirin' o' my talkin',
  And you'd rather list to her'n;
As to me, I'll stick the closer
  To the name upon the stern.

"If she says so, Doctor, take her,
  Keep her. Come here, daughter Ruth.
If she loves ye she will say it —
  She's a girl as speaks the truth."

. . . .

Noontime in Atlantic Basin —
  Sailor lads in greasy dress
Slid from spars of stately traders
  Down the forward hatch to mess.

Rattling chain and creaking tackle
  Smote no longer on the ear;
Dappled sunshine ran in ripples
  On the stringpiece of the pier ;

While the grim old elevators
  Seemed to stop their chronic din
Just to watch two people talking
  On the grain-boat — *Nellie Gwynne.*

THE HORNIN'

WHEN Silas married Rhody Spence,
    Folks thought 'twas kind o' funny;
They argied he was lackin' sense,
    Cos she was lackin' money.

But pretty? Bless ye! She was pink
  An' plump as any pippin ;
An' when she giv' Si' Blois the wink
  She sent three others skippin'.

Now, lots o' girls aroun' our place
  Had set their caps for Silas,
An' 'twixt his money an' her face
  Things seemed to sort o' rile us.

Them was the days when weddin' rings
  Was weighed by friends and minions
An' one might cross an angel's wings
  Before his neighbor's 'pinions.

They had the infare on the hill —
  The house of his Aunt Hanner's.
My! Splendid doin's, dress to kill,
  An' all your comp'ny manners!

But Ransom Hunt, says he to me,
  "There'll be fun yet 'fore mornin'."
She'd mittened Ransom, don't ye see?
  So he got up a hornin'.

Oh, now dew tell! In all the land
  No one blamed Si' fer cursin'.
You'd thought 'twas Satan's cornet band
  Was in the yard rehearsin'!

Fer Ransom bought a big sea-shell
  Would make a graveyard quiver,
An' Dave, his fish horn, we hear well
  When he's daown by the river.

Wes' Pettit beat an old tin pan,
  Some boys was caterwaulin',
An' 'Lijah hitched some dogs as ran
  With strings o' bells a haulin'.

Then folks inside looked queer, ye know,
  An' laughed (behind ther noses);
As fer the bride, a squall o' snow
  Had settled on her roses.

Si' got his gun an' swore he'd shoot
   Until he blowed the end off;
But Hanner cammed him daown real cute,
   Said 'twas a fust-rate send-off.

The horners in the yard had see
   Si' finger with the trigger,
An' got behind an apple tree,
   An' wish't the tree was bigger!

But Silas asked the boys inside —
   They made the sweet-cake shiver —
An' Ransom up an' kissed the bride!
   My, what a smack he giv' her!

Then all arow, an' han' an' toe,
   An' bow low to the fairest;
Across an' back, an' round you go,—
   That reel was jest the rarest!

An' then we left 'em to their choice,
   An' "wish ye joy," sez Ransom.
Si' wan't so bad a feller, boys,
   Now he just come daown hansum!

THEN AND NOW
(For Decoration Day.)

IN haughty and defiant mood,
    With armor flashing, swords upraised,
Majestic, terrible, they stood,
    And in their eyes the anger blazed!

Virginia, beautiful and proud,
Georgia and Texas, starry browed,
Met Massachusetts's azure rays,
And New York's unrelenting gaze.

No words can weigh the woe they made,
    Or measure all the blood that flowed;
Each heard a call, and each obeyed,
    And madly, blindly, onward strode.

What of the men who led them wrong?
    Yet Justice turned their plans to naught;
God touched the scale, the weak grew strong,
    And Freedom's miracle was wrought.

And now the nun-like, soothing years
    Have bound the wounds, the spirits healed,
And who would chase the clouds, the tears,
    When Peace in beauty stands revealed?

The true forbearance and respect,
    The love that levels steeps of hate
Have built again the temple wrecked —
    The harmony that makes us great.

Praise for the South! From bended knee
    She rises now to start anew,
As with a smile, right royally,
    She clasps the hand that overthrew.

But stay! Is there a North or South?
   Who'll give the ground to hold the line
'Twixt mighty Mississippi's mouth
   And snowy Maine's most northern pine?

For with a feeling deep and true,
   In sympathy, at least, to-day,
Fall southern roses o'er the blue,
   And northern violets o'er the gray.

I see the States as if they met
And mingled in the minuet,
Scattering flowers and stepping slow,
While Peace and Love their bugles blow!

For South is North and North is South,
   That which divided binds them round,
And swallows court the cannon's mouth,
   Hid in a honeysuckle mound.

WASHINGTON
(Feb. 22, 1891.)

A MOUNT unmeasured by its peers,
   We trace its shadow hurled,
And say it falls a hundred years
   And reaches round the world!

Our Knight! Of patient, ample mind;
   A form of hero part;
And face so firm it seemed to bind
   The courage of his heart.

No greater in his task divine
   Than great in little things;
'Twas this that made his greatness shine
   Preeminent o'er kings.

On gold and bronze in honored state
   His face for years has shone,
Stamp deeper, day we celebrate,
   His nature on our own.

Had he foreseen what years have brought
   Would he have changed his part?
He bore a nation in his thought —
   Its life-beat in his heart.

GRANT

OUR warrior went to meet the foe
   With good stout heart and steadfast face,
Becoming one with whom did go
   Hopes, prayers, the freedom of a race!

Our warrior played the hero's part,
   Returned the conquered chief his sword,
And won again his humbled heart
   By kindly soldier act and word.

Our warrior met a deadlier foe —
   More grim and terrible than he —
Whose sword was charmed 'gainst any blow,
   Who met his gaze and would not flee.

Oh, dreadful Fate, that overthrew
   The blade that flashed when Vicksburg fell!
Be generous as him you slew;
   Give him the sword he wore so well!

Commissioned now anew, he stands,
   Our Nation's Guard, like adamant;
And swords shall fall from hostile hands,
   When armies shout the name of GRANT.

A KNIGHT OF GOLD
(Tune — "Maryland, My Maryland.")

ON Ohio's prairies wide,
    There Columbia raises
Presidents that give her pride —
    Let us sing their praises!
Garfield, martyr — hero bold,
    Hayes, the true and steady;
McKinley, with a heart of gold,
    Soldiers all and ready!

CHORUS.

Hurrah! then for our warrior bold,
    For he's not plated thinly;
Protection's knight, with mail of gold,
    Invincible McKinley!

Every mountain stream that pours
    Past the spindles flying,
Every ship that leaves our shores,
    Through the billows plying,
Every shepherd with his sheep,
    Sing your praises inly,
Those that delve and those that reap
    Sound your praise — McKinley!

Where Columbia's banner floats
    From ocean unto ocean,
Let us all, by loyal votes,
    Keep it still in motion!
Let us keep her honor bright,
    Keep her credit golden,
While her stars, like gems of light,
    All her sons embolden!

ELECTION DAY

STEADY! Mark time! And forward every man!
　Eyes on the foe, care not for the beholder!
So move to victory like the starry van,
　　Close ranked, resistless, shoulder touching shoulder!

Waterloo, Sedan, and Gettysburg were won
　By armies not so mighty as we bring.
What if we bear a ballot for a gun?
　Yet 'tis the sword and scepter of a king.

Strike straight and strong on Error's hardened pate!
　Strike as they struck, our good colonial sires!
Strike for our Honor, for our Land and State,
　Strike for America and her altar fires!

Steady! Mark time! And forward every man!
　Eyes on the foe, care not for the beholder!
So move to victory like the starry van,
　　Close ranked, resistless, shoulder touching shoulder!

CUBA LIBRE

"CUBA Libre!" Hear our daughter o'er the water bravely cry,
While the smoke that never falters from her altars stains the sky;
While the aged, and the children, and the women stricken, reel:
"Cuba Libre!" is their answer to the tyrant's fatal steel.

"Cuba Libre!" At her option, by adoption, she is ours;
Bound to us by cords of freedom mightier than earthly powers!
She is hoping, she is groping, through the murk of slavery's air.
Shall we by our deafness drive her to the silence of despair?

"Cuba Libre!" shouts Maceo, riding to a martyr's death;
"Cuba Libre!" smiles Bandera, victor in his latest breath!
"Cuba, wilt thou bow thy head? on royal promises rely?"
"Cuba Libre!" Hear a nation saying she would rather die!

"Cuba Libre!" Hear the mountains echo back the patriot boast;
"Cuba Libre!" sing the waves along two thousand miles of coast!
O'er the water hear our daughter saying: "Mother, from thy brow,
I have caught the rays of freedom, you may not disown me now?"

Valiant daughter, o'er the water, we have heard thy moving voice,
And the glory of thy story makes a patriot land rejoice!
Five and forty stars of ours salute thee o'er the tumbling sea,
Pledge their forces in their courses 'til thy single star is free!

A SOLDIER'S SONG

Where the dull wheels jar and jostle,
    And the tramways ring and roar,
Here, like some town-prisoned throstle,
    I have drifted to your door.
Like a bird I wait your giving,
    Like a bird I wait not long,
Song and flight must yield a living
    To a life of flight and song!

Yes, the blue cap, rent and ragged,
    Hardly holds the pennies now;
There in front, that hole so jagged,
    Mates a sword-cut on my brow.
No more war for me! I gladly
    Limp along or stiffly sit,
While the leg I need so badly
    Helps to fill a rifle-pit.

As the echoes climb like lovers,
    Tremble o'er the city's din,
And my song, a lost bird, hovers
    At your window, enters in.
Gentle people, while I linger,
    And my cadences entreat,
Give me, like a feathered singer,
    Bread, for singers fain must eat.

Bread or pennies, e'en a blossom,
    So 'tis thrown with feelings warm,
I will catch as did my bosom
    Bullets in the battle-storm.
Only let the song I send you
    Find you heed a soldier's lay —
Thanks, good lady, God attend you,
    You have brightened all my day!

A SOLDIER'S SONG

Ah, good people, to what other
   Shall I sing the same old song,
Begging pity for a brother
   Maimed in life's remorseless throng?
Shall I tell my heart is longing
   For a music grand and new,
Where the soldier hosts are thronging
   To their Captain's grand review?

PROGRESS

WHAT'S a gem to Irish renters,
   When they want its worth in bread?
What are cars to sick inventors,
   If they jar their dying bed?

Though you gain a proud ascendance
   O'er some theory effete,
Can you sever your dependence
   On the man who sows the wheat?

Does some savant — fossils turning —
   Rank the man who turns the sod?
Can you in the hill of learning
   Burrow out of sight of God?

Progress? Yes, in simple living;
   Love that shines from door to door;
Open lives and secret giving
   For the helping of the poor.

AT GREELEY'S GRAVE
(Greenwood Cemetery, August, 1880.)

THE fountain babbles on the hill,
    The wind among the leaves is sighing
But he is silent, low, and still,
    Beyond this life of toilsome trying.

Fair is the rest he found at length
    Where Nature prints with silent press,
Where oak trees tell his rugged strength
    And blossoms speak his kindliness.

His love of right, his love for men,
    Shed round his name true holiness;
Though kingly with his flashing pen,
    He wore the garb of lowliness.

His own great monument he wrought:—
    The broken fetters of the slave,
The championship of highest thought
    The words he spake, the gifts he gave,

And gratitude from high and low
    His memory will ever grace;
His grand memorial shall grow
    With the uplifting of the race.

So Death brings honors to the brave,
    And Time, at last, is just and true;
The grass is worn about his grave
    By pilgrims whom he never knew.

His spirit lives and speaks again,
    And it shall live in endless youth;
Long as the million hearts of men
    Shall welcome all the words of truth!

AT GREELEY'S GRAVE

Sleep, silent dust, in safety sleep,
   Peacefully rest, secure and still,
Here where the breezes softly sweep,
   And waters murmur on the hill.

INTEGER VITÆ*
President James A. Garfield.
  (Died, Sept. 19, 1881.)

A KIND hand out of reach,
   Silence instead of speech,
  Our greatest heart forever laid at rest;
Only the lesson left
To millions now bereft,
  How grand it is to take Life at its best.

Who has the fitting word,
When every breast is stirred
  With sorrow far too deep for words to tell?
Yet, as amid Death's gloom,
Friends whisper in the room,
  We speak of him who lived and died so well.

Night reigned beside the sea,
When morning came to thee,
  Long-waiting heart, so patient and so brave!
Light fell upon thy door,
Pain ceased forevermore,
  Back to its Maker fled the life He gave.

Like messengers in quest,
Then started east and west
  Two tidal waves of sorrow 'round the world.
Millions of eyes were wet

---

* Horace's " Integer Vitæ " was a favorite poem with President Garfield.

Before the tidings met
  Where in the Eastern seas our flags are furled.

Quickly, through throbbing wire,
Those waves of sorrow dire
  Awoke across the land the mournful bells;
Men roused and could not sleep,
For, pulsing strong and deep,
  All hearts that knew were ringing funeral knells.

Wives gazed in husbands' eyes,
And tears would slowly rise
  For her who fought with Death so long alone;
And children with no task
Were left themselves to ask,
  Why Death this father took, and not their own.

On all the shadow falls.
It hushes college halls,
  It consecrates the cabins of the West;
The freedmen loved him well;
Soldiers his praises tell,
  The rudest boatman is too sad to jest.

From rudest, lowliest ways
To Glory's brightest blaze
  He passed, and threaded all hearts with his love;
True to his humblest friend,
True to life's noblest end,
  True to the God he recognized above.

INTEGER VITÆ

Not in his youthful pride,
Nor in the battle's tide,
   Not in debate when Nations' fates were cast;
But in this gentle sleep
Which he to-day doth keep,
   He won his greatest victory at the last.

Like the One Crucified,
He who so bravely died
   Has made the world the better for his pain;
Surely we now may know
Our leader was laid low
   To lift the Nation to a higher plane.

Still, over hills and dells,
The beautiful, sad bells
   Repeat the Nation's sorrow for her son;
But he doth hear the chime
Of a more peaceful clime
   Than Mentor's fields or quiet Elberon.

We say as once he said —
Our noble ruler dead —
   "The Lord still reigns, the country is secure."
There's none can fill his place.
Rule Thou, O God of grace!
   And guide us on to days more bright and pure.

BOOKS BY THE SAME AUTHOR.

Representative Sonnets by American Poets.

With an Essay on the Sonnet, etc.

BOSTON,

1891.

He has not passed by any single notable sonnet. The essay is a painstaking and valuable monograph. — *New York Evening Post.*

His ear and judgment are alike delicate and accurate. His artistic ideal is high and his expression fortunate. — *Boston Literary World.*

Wayside Music.

Lyrics, Songs, and Sonnets.

NEW YORK,

1893.

He touches the chords of common life with a sincere and tender stroke. — *Syracuse Standard.*

There is a clear, melodious appreciation of verbal music, an ear for the old-time rhythmic swing of English verse. — *New York Commercial Advertiser.*

His poems exhale a breath of that nature of which humanity is itself a part. Dignity and delicacy are equally maintained. — *Philadelphia Evening Bulletin.*

Publishers of *The Century Magazine, Harper's Monthly, The Outlook, The Independent, St. Nicholas, Youth's Companion, Judge, Frank Leslie's Monthly,* New York *Tribune,* Boston *Transcript,* Brooklyn *Standard,* and other newspapers, will please accept thanks for courtesies in regard to reprint of many of the foregoing poems.

The first edition of this book is 500 copies. Printed and bound by L. Barta & Co., Boston.

www.ingramcontent.com/pod-product-compliance
Lightning Source LLC
Chambersburg PA
CBHW031453160426

43195CB00010BB/958